A Woman Who Did Not Wait

A Woman Who Did Not Wait

Louise Odencrantz and Her Fight for the Common Good

Nana Rinehart

Washington, DC

Copyright © 2021 by Nana Rinehart
New Academia Publishing, 2021

All rights reserved. No part of this book may be reproduced or transmitted in any form or by any means, electronic or mechanical, including photocopying, recording, or by any information storage and retrieval system.

Printed in the United States of America

Library of Congress Control Number: 2021921893
ISBN 978-1-7359378-0-9 paperback (alk. paper)

New Academia Publishing, 4401-A Connecticut Ave. NW, #236, Washington, DC 20008
info@newacademia.com - www.newacademia.com

Contents

Acknowledgements	ix
Prologue	1
Chapter I. Pioneer Life	7
Chapter II. Developing a Sense of Identity	17
Chapter III. Discovering Purpose	29
Chapter IV. Fieldwork at the College Settlement	39
Chapter V. Increased Attention to Women Workers	49
Chapter VI. Gaining Professional Recognition	67
Chapter VII. Industry Exists for People	83
Chapter VIII. Connecting Women with Jobs	93
Chapter IX. Finding New Outlets for the Progressive Spirit	111
Chapter X. Life Choices and Relationships	125
Chapter XI. Moving in New Directions	135
Chapter XII. Responding to the Depression	149
Chapter XIII. Finding a Place to Call Home	161
Chapter XIV. Connecting with Danish Relatives and Coping with Old Age	171
Epilogue	179
Notes	183
Bibliography	201
Index	205

Acknowledgements

My greatest debt of gratitude is to the subject of this biography, Louise Odencrantz, who made me feel at home in New York from the moment I arrived there as an exchange student in 1960. Tracing her life and career has given me a sense of connection to the history of the country where I have lived most of my life. I am also grateful to her sister Marguerite, who transcribed and annotated their mother's memoir, to Marguerite's grandson, Todd Stockbauer, who shared these documents with me, and to the grandson of Louise's brother Fred, Kirk Odencrantz, who sent me copies of her water colors.

The Arthur and Elizabeth Schlesinger Library on the History of Women in America, Radcliffe Institute for Advanced Study at Harvard University, provided access to materials on-site and online, which have been essential to the study. Archivists at Barnard College, Columbia University, and Smith College have also been helpful. The Library of Congress collection and the Russell Sage Foundation Archives have been valuable resources.

Throughout the years that I have been working on the book, I have received guidance and encouragement from teachers at the Writer's Center in Bethesda, Maryland, and fellow members of the Washington Biography Group, especially Kenneth Ackerman, Christina Lyons, Patricia McNees, and Sara Taber. Erika Nichols-Frazer reviewed the complete manuscript and offered helpful suggestions. My husband Robert participated in numerous conversations about the biography, read the manuscript in several versions, discussed the content, and gave advice, and my son Benjamin helped format the photographs.

Prologue

Throughout 1912, Louise Odencrantz immersed herself in the crowded neighborhoods of Lower Manhattan doing research for her book on Italian women in industry. Some mornings, she left her office near Washington Square to investigate small workshops in converted residences south of the Square; other days, she walked west along Waverley Place to visit large factory lofts, where heavy sewing machines operated night and day. On the way, she passed the site of the March 1911 Triangle Shirtwaist Factory fire that had killed 146 workers, mostly young women. Many of them had leaped from the ninth floor to their death on the very sidewalk where she walked. Despite the safety measures recommended by the Factory Investigating Commission after the disaster, she found conditions in several workshops similar to those that had caused the fire and the high death toll: piles of debris, locked doors, and inadequate fire escapes. Her focus, however, was not only on the work environment but on the experience of immigrant women laboring under these conditions, many of whom lived in the Italian neighborhood nearby.

To get their perspectives, Louise interviewed individual women in their homes in the evening. After a day of inspecting factories, she entered the dark, littered hallways of neighborhood tenements, climbed grimy wooden stairs, and sat down to talk with her subjects. She loved this part of her work, as she told her Barnard classmates in a booklet prepared for the fifth reunion of the Class of 1907: "What more absorbing than to enter almost into a working girl's life, learn her ways of thinking, her ambitions, her sorrows and worries and her points of happiness? ... There is Jennie, one of my staunch friends. She is an Italian flower maker, 34 years old, who had to go to work when she was 12. 'It must be lovely to know how to read and write,' she said. To you she would appear only a large, stout, cross-eyed woman, ignorant and coarse, but get acquainted!"[1]

Louise had met Jennie while she was living at the College Settlement on the Lower East Side and investigating the conditions of working women in New York for her Columbia University M.A. thesis. She kept in touch with her and others she encountered later while doing similar research for the Russell Sage Foundation, which recognized her skill at gathering and analyzing information and her ability to win the confidence of her subjects. She saw them not just as sociological data but as individual human beings with potential that they might develop if their circumstances were different. At the end of the description of Jennie, she asked "Do you wonder I am a hot suffragist and am willing to wear out the asphalt on Fifth Avenue on May 4th?" She marched in that parade not only because educated women like her Barnard classmates deserved a voice in the nation's affairs, but because she believed that working women like Jennie would be able to change the conditions of their lives if they had the vote.

Although they campaigned for the suffrage, Louise and her peers did not wait for the vote before pushing the limits of what women could do in the public sphere. Curiosity, idealism, and willingness to take risks had motivated her to apply for a fellowship to the College Settlement on Rivington Street. Barnard had nurtured those qualities and given her a sense that she was free to choose the direction of her own life. The first president of the college, Emily Smith Putnam, argued that, "We at Barnard ... are interested in opening every sort of opportunity to women, and then we shall quickly discover what women can do."[2] At the time, women had few professional career options besides teaching, and most graduate programs were closed to them. Louise and others like her did not waste time knocking on locked doors but saw the reality of the world around them—hazardous conditions in New York factories, the tenements where ever-growing numbers of immigrants were living—, recognized the humanity and potential contribution of the people facing these challenges, and campaigned for change. Thus they invented a new profession, variously described as "industrial investigator" or "labor economist"; their goal, however, was not to establish professional identity but to do what needed to be done, solve problems, develop procedures, and look for areas where they could apply their experience. Louise once told an interviewer, "I've always had such fun doing pioneer jobs. It seems to me I never held a job that anybody else had worked out before me."[3]

Throughout her life, Louise saw and embraced diverse possibilities with energy and enthusiasm. After collecting data for the Russell Sage Foundation about industrial conditions and recommending common-sense improvements, she moved on to positions that enabled her to have a direct influence on people's lives. During World War I, she was superintendent of a public employment bureau and helped thousands of women find work, many in non-traditional fields. Later, as personnel manager for a silk manufacturer, she negotiated a strike settlement that satisfied both workers and owners. Always concerned with those on the margins of society, she became an advocate for people with disabilities and directed an agency that expanded their work opportunities. When the Depression struck, she helped coordinate relief efforts and prepared guidelines for the implementation of New Deal policies. Starting each new position, she sized up its problems, applied her experience and imagination to solving them, and left behind guidelines for others before she moved on. She enjoyed being a pioneer and saw each project not only as an adventure in itself, but as part of a larger effort to create a just world.

Pioneering was part of Louise's heritage. Her immigrant parents had homesteaded in Nebraska before moving to Texas and eventually New York. Her Danish mother, Frederikke, was a powerful role model for her daughter. At the age of eighteen, she had left the home of her father, a country vicar, and moved to Copenhagen, where she supported herself as a piano teacher and fell in love with Gustaf, a Swedish music student of aristocratic background. Faced with parental opposition to their marriage, the couple eloped to America in 1879. Frederikke's memoir describing the challenges she and her husband faced as settlers on the prairie shows their courage and resourcefulness. Louise inherited her toughness and combined it with her father's charming manner and ability to get along with people.

I have a personal interest in Louise: She was my grandmother's cousin, and I knew her well during the final decade of her life. While I was in the United States as a Danish exchange student in 1960-61, I spent vacations with her in New York, and I saw her regularly when I returned as a permanent resident a few years later. She had been retired for many years but was keenly interested in current events and active in the Democratic party and in international organizations such as United World Federalists. She had many friends, who treated her with respect and affection. Neither she nor they talked about the work she had done. I did not discover how significant a career she had had until I looked at the papers that she deposited with the Schlesinger Library at Harvard University, including journal and newspaper articles, interviews, and lectures given to professional organizations in the U.S. and Europe.

The Schlesinger Library materials, her contributions to Russell Sage Foundation studies, and other books that she co-authored and published under her own name position Louise among the female researchers and activists who promoted Progressive reform during the first two decades of the twentieth century. Jane Addams (1860-1935), founder of the Hull House Settlement in Chicago, and Florence Kelley (1859-1932), chief factory inspector for Illinois and later head of the National Consumers' League, had defined the Progressive Movement's social justice agenda and opened new professional paths for women. Long before the Nineteenth Amendment gave them the right to vote, these women--and those of a younger generation who followed in their footsteps--exerted considerable influence by raising public awareness of industrial conditions and tenement life and advocating for laws regulating the hours of women workers and for the elimination of child labor.

The most famous of the younger group was Frances Perkins, who became Commissioner of the New York State Department of Labor while Franklin Roosevelt was governor and Secretary of Labor during his presidency. Louise served on committees that advised Perkins in both of these positions and knew many other members of the generation as colleagues and mentors, including Pauline and Josephine Goldmark, who documented the impact on women of long hours and unhealthy working conditions in books and court briefs, and Mary Van Kleeck, who preceded her as a fellow at the College Settlement, supervised her fellowship research, and, later, hired her as a statistician and investigator for the Russell Sage Foundation. During the 1920s, when the federal government abandoned reform efforts, these women continued to implement Progressive principles and practices at the local level and in the private sector, and, during the Depression, they returned these ideas to the mainstream.

Louise and her colleagues believed it was possible to create a better world by gathering facts, listening to all stakeholders, defining shared interests, and building structures that enabled people to meet the challenges facing them. This approach informed her career. She never lost her faith in the common good, worked hard in pursuit of it, and thoroughly enjoyed the effort.

.

Chapter I

Pioneer Life

Early Childhood in Nebraska

"I have always had a deep and powerful yearning for a place I could call home. But I have an equally deep and powerful desire for what lies beyond the horizon. Perhaps it is because the horizons I knew as a boy in Nebraska never really closed the landscape but invited one to what lay beyond."[1] Louise copied that passage from Alvin Johnson, *Pioneers' Progress,* on the back of a letter from the American Association for the United Nations about peaceful use of atomic energy. The two sides of that piece of paper mark the starting and end points of her journey from the little house on the prairie that was her first home to her career in New York and her effort to realize what lay beyond the horizon—a humane, inclusive, and peaceful world.

Her younger sister Marguerite described Louise's progress in less lofty terms: "Don't think you're so important! You were born in a sod hut," she used to joke when they were both adults. Actually, that was not quite true. According to Frederikke Odencrantz' memoir,[2] the house that she and her husband built "stood on a high rise [later known as 'the Odencrantz Table'] and could be seen for miles around on the vast sea of the prairie." It was a "roomy and comfortable" frame house "of the best lumber obtainable," with plastered walls, and it had space for the piano, organ, other musical instruments, and the book collection that the couple had brought with them when they immigrated from Scandinavia. The quality of the house and its contents reflected their middle- and upper-class backgrounds. They had come to America not because they were poor and desperate but because they were looking for opportunities to invest their resources and apply their talents. After living in Chicago for four years, they responded to the Swede Olof Bergström's promotion of a settlement named "Gothenburg" in Nebraska, where they acquired a 160-acre homestead and purchased another 160 acres. In the summer of 1883, they moved west with their three-year-old daughter Tulla. Three other children were born in Nebraska—Louise in 1884, Fred in 1886, and Marguerite in 1888.

Louise was too young to experience the challenges that her parents faced as settlers on the prairie, but she listened to her mother's tales, and the narrative blended with her own early childhood recollections. Years later, Marguerite described how Frederikke used to sit in her rocking chair and, with dramatic emphasis, tell stories to her attentive grandson, who occasionally exclaimed, "Oh no, Grandma, you didn't!" One can imagine similar scenes in the Odencrantz family a generation earlier, the children at their mother's feet, listening to her tales of the cyclone that carried off her laundry and the partly-built stable; the brush fire that would have destroyed the house if a sudden cloudburst had not saved it; and the time when Tulla and Frederikke, pregnant with Louise, would have perished in the cold while Gustaf was away if a neighbor had not come to their rescue after noticing that no smoke was rising from the chimney; and the armed men on horseback that showed up one dark night asking for food and shelter and who, Gustaf later learned, were suspected of murdering other settlers. He had found them to be very polite: They had brought him a freshly killed deer, which they cut up and salted because he did not know what to do with it, and before leaving, they had listened to their hosts' performance of piano duets. (Frederikke wrote down these stories later; Marguerite transcribed them, adding recollections of her own, and destroyed most of the manuscripts; a few original hand-written fragments survive, suggesting that, at least by the time she set down her recollections, Frederikke's English was fluent.)

Music was another source of entertainment for the children during dark evenings in the little house; the parents were both classically trained musicians, who had met while they were studying in Copenhagen. Frederikke was probably more accomplished than Gustaf, but his playing was fun: "He was always good at improvising, and he would play for us with great gusto and many flourishes," Marguerite recalled. Throughout their childhood, the children were also surrounded by the books that the Odencrantzes had brought with them. "Our home became a sort of gathering place for the settlers who were rapidly taking up claims around us," Frederikke wrote. "When anyone wanted a book, we were glad to let them borrow it. Few of our neighbors, however, could read English, and those who could read but slowly. All of them were Scandinavians, and we had books in those languages too."

Frederikke was able to laugh at the mistakes she made as a newcomer, unfamiliar with the fauna and flora of the prairie. Once, she tried to trap a skunk in order to send it to the Chicago Zoo because it looked so cute with its bushy striped tail; another time, she planted a beautiful vine and trained it to grow up the wall of the house—until a neighbor told her it was poison ivy. Louise inherited her mother's sense of humor as well as her persistence and willingness to find new solutions to problems. The lack of water was a major issue for the settlers. Although neither Frederikke nor Gustaf had ever seen a cistern, they decided to build one with the help of their carpenter. The men dug a hole big enough to hold thirty barrels while she carried off the earth that they sent up in buckets. "They made it a square instead of the usual round shape and cemented it carefully," she wrote in her memoir, proudly adding, "this cistern took a long time to construct, but it proved to hold water better than the larger round ones that were built by professionals." She also determined to get the better of a cow, which kept kicking over the pail when she was being milked: "Early one morning, taking the pail and a small switch, I went out to where she was tied. Showing her the switch, I laid it on the ground in front of her where she could keep it in view. I talked nicely to her, telling her she was a good cow, and that if she behaved well, I would not use the switch. Then I started to milk her. She stood still long enough for me to get quite a bit of milk."

Milk was a staple of the children's diet, supplemented with eggs from the chickens, corn from the fields, and home-preserved vegetables. Sugar, flour and bacon were shipped from Chicago along with canned goods, but they never had fresh fruit, only dried prunes and apples. Despite the limited diet, they were healthy—

perhaps because they came in contact with very few people who might transmit colds or other diseases. In the summer, they played outdoors most of the time, unsupervised, with broken dishes, mud, grass, chicken feathers, and cast-off snake rattles. Decades later, Louise visited crowded tenements in New York, where young immigrant children spent their days gluing petals on artificial flowers to earn money for their families, in striking contrast to the freedom and open air she enjoyed as a child.

Once, when she was about two, Louise wandered off from the place just outside the house where she usually played, and nobody could find her when it was time for supper. She herself would have remembered the incident vaguely if at all, but her mother later told how she searched frantically for her little girl while the sun was setting and the coyotes beginning to howl until she finally found her "between the rows of the tall corn, just awakening, now crying, her face covered with mud from tears and dirt. She smiled when she saw me. She had been fast asleep, tired from running and crying." Frederikke concluded the story by citing the hired man, who said he was sure little Louise went toward the cornfield because she had heard him calling "git up" to the horses. When she wrote her account of that event many years after it occurred, was Frederikke thinking about the ways in which her daughter had followed the call to "git up" and move on?

Busy as she was, Frederikke tried to provide treats for her children. In the summer, she made "lemonade" out of sugar, vinegar, and water. When Christmas came, she searched in vain for presents at the village store, which sold only groceries. All she could come up with were little knick-knacks that she had brought from Denmark. She placed them under the tree and let the children play with them for a few days before she put them away for another holiday. After a couple of years, they caught on, and she had to think of something else. She did not mention what she got for the younger children, but she bought a slate and a stylus for Tulla, which were a great success: "It actually started her off on arithmetic. We could never give her long enough or difficult enough sums to do. She would sit by the kitchen stove working on these while I cooked the dinner. She became a mathematics teacher when she finished her education."

Frederikke and Gustaf were anxious about their children's education. She regretted that she had only been taught at home by a governess and envied the children in the Danish village where she grew up because they were allowed to study and play together and gained much better skills than she and her sister: "When it came to arithmetic, beautiful script, singing and doing athletic stunts, the peasant boys and girls beat us many times over," she used to say. But her own children's only option was a school in Gothenburg twenty miles away—too far to travel every day—until she and Gustaf helped start a school near their home. They raised $40 to hire a teacher, a girl of fourteen who had finished the fourth grade, and provided room and board for her during the two months of the year that the school was open. A neighbor offered a sod house as a classroom for Tulla, Louise, and the four other children that attended.

Providing better educational options for the children was one reason why Gustaf and Frederikke considered a move. Having cultivated the homestead for more than five years and become American citizens, they were able to claim the original grant without having to live on it. They decided to let the land along with the house and other parcels that they had purchased to a neighboring farmer and move into Gothenburg, where Gustaf would open a shop. Before they moved, they made a fifty-mile trip across the Sand Hills to North Platte in order to have a photograph taken of the family that they could send to relatives in Scandinavia. It was the first time the children had travelled farther than the twenty miles to Gothenburg, and Frederikke and Gustaf turned the trip into an adventure. They borrowed a wagon big enough to carry the whole family, their bedding, food, and the dress clothes they would wear for the photo. The first night they camped out, keeping dry under the wagon cover despite a heavy downpour, but the next day, after a difficult trek through the Sand Hills when wagon wheels kept getting stuck, they arrived at a house—the home of Mrs. Cody, the wife of Buffalo Bill, who invited them to spend the night. "Mrs. Cody was a dressmaker and later on used to help me make the children's clothes," Frederikke wrote. The family enjoyed the five-day outing and "the photographs were a great success, very much appreciated by our relatives back in Europe."

Although the Odencrantz family looked forward to the move to Gothenburg, the following description, written many years later, suggests that Frederikke left her home on the prairie with some regret: "This land of ours, where we had built our house, was called the high-table land with the rolling prairies. These rolling prairies resembled very much the waves of the ocean, especially toward evening when the shadows became longer. They were very beautiful, not flat and monotonous like the prairie near the railroad. They would form pictures different from one day to the other. I loved to sit on the kitchen stoop when my work was done and try to make out these different pictures so I would never forget them." Louise was not yet six years old when she left her first home, but her saving of the Alvin Johnson quote implies that the landscape of her childhood had left a deep impression on her.

Family photo. Tulla is standing behind Frederikke, who has Marguerite on her lap. Fred is in the middle, and Louise is leaning against Gustaf.

Small-Town Life

Gothenburg had grown considerably from the few houses next to the whistle stop on the Pacific Railroad where Gustaf and Frederikke had arrived six years earlier. The number of inhabitants was approaching 500, and Main and Front Streets were lined with houses and paved—with a compact mixture of sand and manure from the livery stable. In December 1889, Gustaf opened his store on Front Street and, according to Marguerite, stocked it with everything from pianos, organs and other musical instruments to chewing gum. When the holiday merchandise arrived, eager customers seized the articles as soon as he opened the packing crates—even before he could put on price tags. Frederikke probably salvaged a few items to put under the family's tree that Christmas. The *Gothenburg Times* covered the event, showing a photo of "G. Odencrantz, the musical man of the town, in front of his store that handles pianos and other musical instruments."

Besides selling musical instruments, Gustaf and Frederikke offered music lessons to customers. They also assumed an active role in the cultural and civic life of the town. In November 1891, she and another pianist gave a recital at a new concert hall, which netted $60 for a fund that Gustaf had organized in order to buy a fire engine, the first piece of fire-fighting equipment owned by the town. Later he gave a concert of his own to purchase 100 yards of fire hose. After the lonely years on the prairie, he and Frederikke enjoyed being among people and participating in community activities. Civic responsibility was part of the heritage they passed on to their children.

The Odencrantz children attended the local school, which had separate teachers for the lower and upper grades. Louise's experience there was not entirely happy, however. In order to "cure" her left-handedness, the teacher tied her left hand behind her back, forcing her to use her right hand, which she did for the rest of her life, but her hand-writing was always awkward. Her papers include a water color, which she copied and signed; it shows a very unhappy little girl, grasping her slate, and carries the caption "And they say school days are your happiest days."

The family lived in rooms behind the store in a space that was probably more confining than the house they came from, and, when spring arrived, the children must have missed playing outside in the open fields. After the initial excitement of starting the business, Gustaf, who was always restless, found the daily task of running it tedious. He and Frederikke had come to America in the hope of making their fortune, but the number of pianos they could sell and lessons they could give in a town with 500 inhabitants was unlikely to yield that result. A friend invited him to visit Texas to explore possibilities there, and, when he returned, he told his children about the strawberries, the enormous watermelons, and other wonders of the place. He might also have heard rumors about oil exploration although the Texas oil boom did not really start until 1894. Meanwhile, Nebraska suffered protracted droughts and crop failures during the 1890s, and land prices dropped. The national panic of 1893—the most severe depression yet experienced by the United States—aggravated the situation. It looked like a good time to get out and try something else.

Facing New Challenges in Texas

In 1894, when Louise was ten years old, Gustaf and Frederikke hired a freight car to hold their possessions—furniture, pianos and other instruments, books, and music—and set off for Houston. One can imagine the excitement of the children as they boarded the train, whose whistle they had heard every day when it passed through Gothenburg, leaving behind the only world they knew. Their parents had told them about Houston, a city with 40,000 inhabitants, where there would be a demand for piano lessons because people were interested in music; Houston had several choral groups and a Philharmonic Society that gave regular performances. Most importantly, the city had a free public high school—one of the first in the country—which Tulla would enter immediately.

After a while, Gustaf decided to leave the music instruction to Frederikke and purchased ten acres of land in Webster, a small rural community with about 200 inhabitants, twenty miles south of Houston. Frederikke remained in the city, teaching increasing numbers of pupils, who were attracted by accounts in local papers of student recitals at her home, and earning a steady income that would support her husband's new farming venture. Tulla stayed with her mother to attend high school, and the three younger children moved to Webster with Gustaf, who began raising fruit and vegetables on the small farm. The train between Houston and Galveston stopped at Webster, making it possible for Tulla and Frederikke to join the rest of the family on weekends and during vacations.

Water supply was a problem in Texas as it had been in Nebraska; Gustaf kept barrels on the roof to collect rain water for washing and for watering the orchard but had to fetch drinking water from the Artesian well one mile from the farm. The children, however, enjoyed the access to fresh fruit: "Figs were plentiful on our small farm in Webster. We gathered the ripe, purple figs in dishpans early in the morning before the birds got them. We also had persimmons, but how they puckered our mouths if we ate them before they were ripe," Marguerite recalled. They also picked watermelons, which they dropped on the ground to split open so that they could eat the ripe, red middle, and they learned to enjoy "the fat okra Mama put in the ham gumbo, which made it slimy but delicious." When the sisters walked back from school, they stopped to pick apples and berries and had part of their lunch before they got home.

Marguerite and Fred ran barefoot all summer, "which probably made our feet and ankles strong since both of us became good ice skaters in later years. ... The big red ants, almost an inch long, stung our bare feet, [and] Mother extracted wood ticks from our bare backs with a sterile needle." Other insects caused problems as well. The legs of tables, chairs and bureaus had to be placed in cans of kerosene to prevent ants from crawling up, and, although everybody slept under mosquito nets, Louise and her father caught malaria. The doctor prescribed quinine in dry powder form, which seems to have cured hers, but he had recurrent attacks of chills, fever, and body pain.

Malaria was not the only reason why life in Texas may have been difficult for Louise. Although she was only eleven years old when her mother decided to stay in Houston, she assumed responsibility for looking after her younger siblings and coping with household chores. The school in Webster was even smaller than the one in Gothenburg; a local history mentions that, in 1905, it had forty-four pupils and one teacher. Did she miss Nebraska? Perhaps the longing for a place to call home that she found in the Alvin Johnson quote had its origin in this and other disruptions during her childhood. She probably felt lonely; her younger siblings played together, but her home duties left her little time for playing or making friends. Eventually, by the time she was fourteen, she started high school (her papers include a "certificate of achievement" from the Houston normal school), but it is not clear whether she stayed with her mother in the city or took the train in from Webster, and she left no record of her activities during this time. Her accent, however, would carry traces of Texas as well as Nebraska—even after decades of residence in New York.

The Texas adventure ended suddenly. One day in late May 1899, Marguerite came home from school, looking forward to the free ice cream soda that a downtown shop was offering—the first ever in the region—but she never got her treat. Her father greeted her with the message that his widowed mother had died; the family would need to go to Sweden as soon as possible to settle the estate and take care of other matters. The children had heard their parents talk about leaving Texas because of the effect of the climate on Gustaf's health, but the grandmother's death precipitated a decision. Frederikke gave notice to her music pupils and returned from Houston to prepare for the departure by booking passage to Europe, ordering mourning clothes for the children, putting the family's most important belongings in storage, and selling the rest since, whatever they decided to do in the future, they would not return to Texas.

Chapter II

Developing a Sense of Identity

Connecting with Scandinavia

The Odencrantz family boarded a ship in Galveston and sailed through the Gulf of Mexico and along the East Coast to New York, where they transferred to the Scandinavian-American liner that would carry them across the Atlantic. "We had all kinds of weather on that long trip," especially on the last leg of the journey through the choppy North Sea; everybody onboard got seasick, but "Papa never lost a meal," Marguerite proudly recorded.[1]

The long journey provided opportunities for the children to hear again the familiar stories about their parents' childhood and youth, which held new interest now that they were about to visit the old countries. They had grown up looking at the portraits of Gustaf's mother and Frederikke's father that hung in the living room.[2] The elder Mrs. Odencrantz looked stern and dignified in a high-collared black dress and a lace cap tied under her chin, but she and her husband (a retired army officer of aristocratic background, who died a few years before his wife) had been indulgent parents to their only son. After graduating from the college-preparatory "gymnasium" in Uppsala, he had studied law for a while; when he tired of that, they bought a farm for him, and he tried his hand at agriculture until he decided that what he really wanted to do was study music in Copenhagen, where he had met his future wife. Frederikke's father, Ole Aarestrup Smith, the Lutheran pastor in a village on the Danish island of Funen, looked gentle and a little distant in the portrait that Louise inherited. He was fifty-four when his daughter was born; between his pastoral duties and his passionate interest in music, he did not have much time for her, but she remembered helping him cultivate asparagus in the large rectory garden.

Listening to their mother's vivid, unsentimental accounts, the children must have absorbed knowledge about the home she had left and recognized the strong personality that she displayed even as a ten-year-old. Growing up with three older brothers, she had learned early to stand up for herself: "The [1864] war between Denmark and Germany was being fought close to our island. What they were fighting about I did not know, but I guess they did. When I fought, I knew why—for example, when my brothers stole the pears that I had picked early in the morning, long before they were up, and hidden under a gooseberry bush." She also had a strong sense of responsibility for her community and took part in a volunteer effort to supply Danish soldiers with hand-knit socks: "I could knit one big sock in two evenings, turning the heel and finishing off the toe all by myself. I knew that, if I did not handle the long needles fast enough, our country and homes might be lost."[3] Louise inherited her spirit of service and her practical approach. Both mother and daughter looked at the world around them, found ways to solve problems, and enjoyed being part of the process.

Frederikke passed on to her children her resentment that her parents had invested all their resources in the future of their sons. They had helped the eldest purchase a large farm in northern Jutland, where the youngest joined him to help out and learn agriculture. A third son studied medicine in Copenhagen and later practiced as a doctor in a town near his brother. According to the notes that Marguerite added to the transcript of her mother's memoirs, the family had to "skimp and save so there would be enough money for her eldest brother's farm, where he and his attractive young bride were trying to make a go of it." When Pastor Smith retired, he moved with his wife and daughters to the town of Svendborg, where Frederikke took piano lessons from a teacher, whose skills she soon surpassed. Her future looked like a choice between marrying one of the young men in the little town or staying home to take care of her aging parents, but, as Marguerite wrote, "Mother was always lucky." Her grandmother won a large sum in the Danish State Lottery and shared it with Frederikke, who decided to use the money to fund her further musical education in Copenhagen. In 1872, at the age of eighteen, despite her parents' objections, she left home for the big city, setting an example of independence that her own daughters would follow.

The study of music was one of the few advanced education options available to women, who were not admitted to the University of Copenhagen until 1875 and did not have access to academic secondary schools. Frederikke took private lessons with professors from the Conservatory, which she paid for by giving lessons to beginners, and, by the time she met Gustaf, she had been supporting herself for several years. Marguerite described Gustaf and Frederikke as an unlikely couple: "Pappa was a tall, handsome man with large brown eyes. He was a great jollier and had a way with women. Mother was short and rather plump, with large blue eyes and long blond braids, which she coiled around her head like a crown" (in the same style that Louise later adopted).

Portrait of Frederikke as a young woman in Copenhagen

The portrait shows Frederikke's intelligent, determined face, her long braid, and her stocky figure, somewhat camouflaged by the then-fashionable bustle. The strength of her character may have been part of her attraction for Gustaf, who would depend on her steadying influence for sixty years. Both sets of parents objected to the match—his because she was not an aristocrat, hers because he was a foreigner. The young couple might eventually have persuaded their parents to accept their spouses, but both were restless and adventurous. Copenhagen was full of agents advertising the increased speed and comfort of technically advanced steamships and promoting the opportunities offered by the United States. 170,000 Danes and an even greater number of Swedes left for the new world during the last three decades of the nineteenth century. Gustaf and Frederikke saw emigration as a solution to their problem. They booked passage on a British steamer out of Liverpool and set off to seek fame and fortune in America and thus overcome their families' opposition. Although they stayed in touch with them, they never saw their parents again.

Twenty years later, Gustaf and Frederikke were returning to Scandinavia with their four children. After nine-and-a-half days on the Atlantic and the North Sea, they disembarked and caught the train to Linköping. The children must have found the cobbled streets of Gustaf's hometown and its towered medieval cathedral very different from their surroundings in rural Texas, where, a few weeks before, they had been roaming the countryside. Now, wearing the mourning clothes that Frederikke had ordered for them out of respect for the grandmother they had never seen, they had to move carefully among the heirloom furniture in the dark, high-ceilinged rooms of her house, minding their manners, and remembering to greet adults with a curtsey or a bow. Their grandmother's housekeeper had kept everything in perfect shape for their arrival, but she did not take kindly to fingerprints on the furniture she had polished so carefully. It was a challenging cultural encounter, but it gave the children insights into their father's background.

The children's knowledge of their parents' native tongues was minimal. Gustaf and Frederikke might have spoken Swedish and Danish with each other initially (the two languages are close enough that, with a little practice, speakers of one can understand the other), but gradually English became the language of the Odencrantz household. Fortunately, one of Gustaf's s few living relatives, his cousin Jeanette, spoke excellent English. She became a special friend of Louise's, and she may have been the first to introduce the idea of attending college to the young girl from rural Texas. The two of them continued corresponding after the visit. In a 1904 letter, Jeanette thanked Louise for a picture of Barnard College (where she was in the middle of her first year) and hoped for further reports of her activities: "It gives me always a great pleasure to hear how my young relation is studying and how you are amusing yourself; oh, you will be very profoundly learned in a short time."[4] The letter mentioned that Jeanette had just read "a very amusing book, *The History of the United Netherlands* by Motley," which suggests her academic interests. Jeanette was probably "the pioneering aunt," mentioned in an article about Louise in 1916, who had been "one of the first women to take the degree of doctor of philosophy at a Swedish university."[5] She was also an accomplished artist and may have encouraged her young relative to try her hand at water-colors.

After two months in Sweden, Frederikke took her children to Denmark while Gustaf stayed behind to wind up his affairs. They stopped in Copenhagen, which had expanded considerably during the final decades of the nineteenth century. Frederikke recognized some of the landmarks such as the Cathedral and the Royal Theater, but many elegant new buildings, inspired by Parisian models, had been built since she left. It was the first major city that Louise ever visited. She bought a collection of post-card-size pictures showing monuments, churches, theaters, and open squares dotted with gentlemen in top hats and ladies in long skirts carrying parasols, and wrote her name on the cover, "L. Odencrantz, 1899."

From Copenhagen, Frederikke and her children took the train and ferry to the city of Odense on Funen to call on the widow of her eldest brother, in whose ventures their parents had invested so heavily. He had died a few months earlier after losing his farm and fortune, leaving his widow and five children financially dependent on her brother, in whose home they were living. One of the Danish children, my grandmother Marianne, remembered opening the door, seeing her aunt and four cousins lined up on the stairs outside, and wondering how they were all going to fit into the modest apartment. The start of the visit was awkward: Frederikke had come to claim her share of the inheritance from her father, which had been left in her brother's charge, and it had been a challenge for the widow to extricate the amount owed. Gradually, however, the tension eased. Louise made friends with Marianne, her near contemporary, and showed her the pictures of Copenhagen that she had bought. Before she left, she gave the booklet to her cousin, who saved it for the rest of her life as a memento of the encounter. None of the Danes spoke English, but Frederikke was able to interpret and probably entertained her nephews and nieces with stories about her life in America. Perhaps this was when the idea of emigrating first captured the imagination of eighteen-year-old Louis and fourteen-year-old Soren, both of whom left for New York a few years later. The two families stayed in touch after the visit.

The visit to Scandinavia gave Louise a new sense of identity. She developed an understanding of her roots in Sweden and Denmark and her connections to relatives there, but she had no doubt that her future would be in America—although she was not sure where exactly her parents would find a new home. They would definitely not return to Texas because of the climate, and rural Nebraska offered no educational opportunities. Finally, they decided they would go to Chicago, where they had lived for four years when they first arrived in the United States. Louise must have wondered why. She knew that they had left that city because they were unhappy there and attributed the death of their second daughter Petra in 1883 to its unhealthy conditions. But they were familiar with Chicago and knew that it had a large Swedish population (until 1960, Swedes ranked as the city's fifth-largest foreign-born group), who would provide music students for Frederikke and customers for the store that Gustaf planned to open. At the end of the summer, they booked passage on a liner bound for New York, from where they would take the train to Chicago.

Putting Down Roots in New York

When the Odencrantz family arrived in New York in early October 1899, Gustaf had another malaria attack, from which he recovered faster than ever before. He and Frederikke concluded that New

York provided a healthier environment than Chicago and decided to remain—an abrupt decision with far-reaching consequences. As soon as he was well enough, they began exploring housing options. The Bronx had recently become a borough of New York City, connected to Manhattan by the Third Avenue El, and was being developed to accommodate the city's expanding population. There they found an apartment and moved in, arranging for their furniture, piano, books, and household goods stored in Houston to be sent by rail. What a difference from their previous home: No need to sleep under mosquito nets, place saucers of kerosene underneath the furniture, or collect rainwater on the roof for bathing—you just turned on the tap, and the water flowed!

One reason why the Odencrantz family chose the Bronx may have been the fact that one of the three public high schools created by the New York City School Reform Act of 1896 was located there. Known initially as the "Mixed High School" because it was co-educational, it was later named Morris High School. When Gustaf visited the institution, he was impressed that the Latin teacher pronounced the language like his teacher at *gymnasium* in Uppsala. (According to her portrait in the 1904 school yearbook, Miss Josie A. Davis was also an attractive young woman with gently curling hair and beautiful eyes, which may have influenced him as well.) Although the school year had begun almost two months before, he persuaded the principal, Dr. Edward Jasper Goodwin, to admit Louise to the ninth grade. She had been out of school since May and faced the challenge of catching up with her peers, but on her very first day, she made a friend, whom she would stay in touch with for the rest of her life, Mary O'Hara. (Marguerite mentioned in a 1964 letter that Mary had shared Thanksgiving Dinner with her and Louise.)

Louise was fortunate to attend what might have been one of the best public schools in the country. Dr. Goodwin was a charismatic leader and educational reformer, who saw the goal of high school as social and intellectual development rather than the accumulation of information. He advocated the use of the project method and the inclusion of electives in the curriculum, and he believed that teachers needed to be "cultured, broadminded and socially responsive," and have a strong academic foundation in the subjects they taught.

90 percent of Morris High faculty had bachelor degrees (compared with the national norm of 50 percent), many from major universities and colleges.[6]

The magnificent building designed for Morris High School, which is now on the Register of Historic Buildings, did not open until after Louise had graduated; throughout her high-school years, classes were held on the top floor of an elementary school on 157th Street. The cramped quarters did not hamper school spirit, however. A member of the Class of 1904 described his experience fondly: "That little old school house recalls pleasant thoughts. It was presided over by Dr. Edward J. Goodwin, beloved by teachers and pupils alike. How fatherly he ruled, yet how sternly! ... Two things stand out clearly—one, the intimate and personal relations that existed between pupils and teachers. ...The other thing that stands out is the school spirit. Our school—how we loved it, how we worked for it, how we cheered our leaders on."[7]

Louise's older sister Tulla, who had graduated from high school in Houston, entered Columbia Teachers College in 1900. Fred and Marguerite, who enrolled in local elementary schools, probably missed the freedom to roam the countryside that they had had in Texas. Marguerite acquired a pair of roller skates, which enabled her to cruise the sidewalks of the neighborhood. Fred used to hang out at a factory near their home, where he would sit on a high railing watching other boys playing. They were a raucous lot, and, on one occasion, they made such a nuisance of themselves that the factory owner called the police. The big boys took off, but Fred did not get away in time, and the police brought him to the station and contacted his home. Marguerite returned from roller-skating in time to see her "rotund little mother with determined small steps" bringing her son back. "He'll just have to learn to run faster," was her only comment, but later she reported to the family that she had told the police they would do better if they spent their time catching burglars than arresting little boys. "Knowing Mother I bet she told them," Marguerite added.[8]

That incident may have contributed to the family's decision to look for a new home. Realtors had built brownstone homes and apartments in West Harlem in the hope of attracting middle-class residents; when demand failed to match supply, they lowered rents. The Odencrantzes found an apartment on West 122nd Street in a neighborhood now designated the Mount Morris Park Historic District. It was more expensive than the flat in the Bronx, but Gustaf had opened a book-store, supplementing the rental income from the Nebraska and Texas properties and the return on the investment of their inheritance, which had supported the family in the initial phase of the New York life. The new apartment had more space than any of their previous homes and could accommodate the heirlooms from Gustaf's childhood home in Sweden, which had been shipped to America. The living room provided a cozy setting for family musical evenings and a place where Frederikke could teach the piano students she began to acquire.

The street outside was lined with trees, and the steep, rocky terrain of Mount Morris Park (renamed Marcus Garvey Park in 1973) only two blocks away could make you forget you were in the city. Frederikke liked to pose family pictures there, which she sent to her Danish relatives. She also included a photo of Gustaf with the rowboat he acquired. On Sundays, he often took her and the children out on the Hudson River. "I never saw a better oarsman than Pappa at fifty years of age; he pulled the boat with the whole family of six in it, with strong and fast strokes," Marguerite proudly claimed.

Gustaf was 58 in this photo, which Frederikke sent to her Danish sister-in-law.

The move to West Harlem meant a long daily commute for Louise. In order to catch the Third Avenue El, which stopped a block from her school, she had to travel by streetcar through East Harlem, which housed thousands of recently arrived southern Italians and Sicilians. This was the first neighborhood in New York known as "Little Italy," a name later given to other areas including the one that would become the focus of her research a few years later. From the carriage window, she would have seen decrepit tenement buildings, pushcarts lining the streets, and sidewalks crowded with pedestrians of all ages. Observing the contrast between those scenes and her home in West Harlem, where middle-class families lived in dignified houses with modern conveniences, must have been a formative experience. As Nicholas Butler, president of Columbia University, said, "The great city, and especially New York, is intensely cosmopolitan, and contact with its life ... during the impressionableness of youth is in itself a liberal education."[9]

At Morris High School, Louise followed the "Classical Course," which prepared students for admission to elite colleges. It included four years of English, Latin, and math; three years of history and either Greek, French, or German; plus a year of "physiology" and a year of either physics or chemistry. Over a period of five days in June 1903, she took the entrance exam for Barnard. The standard was high. For English, "the candidate is expected to read intelligently all the books prescribed ... [and] to have freshly in mind their most important parts ... a considerable amount of English poetry should be committed to memory." The history exam demanded specific knowledge as well as analytic skills: "Show how far Lincoln's phrase 'government of the people, by the people, for the people' can be applied to [either] Athenian democracy [or] the Roman Republic."[10] In addition to the required subjects, Louise took advanced tests in Latin, including Cicero, Virgil, advanced composition, and sight translation. The Barnard scholarship committee reviewed her blue books and awarded her a grant for the full annual tuition of $150.

Frederikke had won a lottery when she was eighteen, which enabled her to go to Copenhagen to study music. Her daughter was even more fortunate, having arrived in New York just as the first public high schools opened and gained admission to an elite institution through a competitive entrance exam. She was fortunate as well in having parents who had the financial means to support her while she attended college and left her free to choose her own path. Most middle- and upper-class parents at the time saw marriage as their daughters' primary goal in life and discouraged anything that might get in the way, such as higher education. Frederikke and Gustaf had chosen to leave their homes for an uncertain future in the new world, and their only expectation for their children was that they make the most of the opportunities it offered.

Chapter III

Discovering Purpose

The Barnard Experience

A student arriving at Barnard in the fall of 1903 might almost forget that she was in New York City. The landscape surrounding the college was still rural: "To the south of the Barnard quadrangle lay an open expanse of fields. On the north stretched a similar tract, rather rocky, and inhabited by goats," according to an early description. Riverside Drive was being developed, but the apartments that would block the view of the Hudson River had not gone up, and "the western sun sinking behind New Jersey's Palisades was an evening pageant which stirred many generations of Barnard women."[1]

The college was expanding, however. Construction had recently begun on several new buildings between 116th and 119th Streets along Broadway, and Louise's class of 100 was the largest in the school's history. Despite the bucolic surroundings, Barnard was part of the city, and students were expected to blend in and dress properly. During orientation, the Undergraduate Association reminded them that they must wear hats outside at all times except when heading to the playing field for physical education and sports.[2]

To get to the campus from her parents' home in West Harlem, Louise had to take the streetcar across town on 125th Street north of Central Park and transfer to Ninth Avenue El, which had a stop three quarters of a mile from the campus. The majority of Barnard undergraduates commuted from the greater New York City area and thus represented a wider range of social classes than students at other women's colleges. Daughters of parents who could not afford to send them away to institutions where they had to pay room and board chose Barnard, as did young women from prominent families, who had to maintain their position in society by attending balls and other functions during the winter season. A college historian notes that "the mingling of these two groups was instructive to both. It produced a combination of polish and practicality which gave Barnard its own distinctive flavor from the first."[3] A number of students attended on full-tuition academic scholarships—including Louise and Agnes Ernst, her classmate from Morris High School. (Agnes gained recognition on campus as an athlete and student leader; later she married financier Eugene Meyer, who acquired the *Washington Post,* and became an influential public figure.) Students who developed financial need after enrolling could apply for scholarships from the Student Loan Committee of the Alumnae Association.

The school's diversity was religious as well as social: While other women's colleges "drew their students overwhelmingly from Protestant families, Barnard also attracted the daughters of Jews and Catholics."[4] The mingling of different groups and the fact that the institution was never cut off from the larger metropolitan area gave the school its special atmosphere. A student who had transferred from a college in New England found that Barnard had "considerably less of that 'bluestocking' deadly seriousness than prevailed in the other college. There was a liberating atmosphere of humor, balance, and common sense at Barnard." Those qualities would have made Louise feel at home immediately, and so would the idea—articulated by Emily Smith Putnam, the first head of Barnard—that for women to engage in higher education "against the will of the world" was an adventure.[5]

The agreement that Putnam had negotiated with Columbia confirmed Barnard's status as an independent college for women with its own endowment, administration, and faculty but gave students access to the University's upper-level courses and libraries. Requirements at the two institutions were similar: "The Barnard student and her brother at Columbia were required to spend about half of their four years in various courses, but they were also required on graduation to know one thing pretty well."[6]

Professors set high standards for their students. Alice Duer Miller recalled how Professor William T. Brewster challenged his English composition class: "Many an alumna can shut her eyes, and see those themes coming back with terse comments in red ink, in Mr. Brewster's hand-writing: 'Trite,' 'Lacking in unity,' 'What of it' ... comments very different from the gentle, encouraging amenities of school-day compositions, and much more stimulating to fresh endeavors."[7] Louise's books and articles show that she benefited from Mr. Brewster's advice such as "choose concrete subjects," and "places must be visualized."

Louise's Latin professor Dr. Charles Knapp, a noted classical scholar, regarded his students as intellectual equals, telling them "that he and they were alike travelers on the road of learning, and the space between them was so small, in comparison with the length of the road, that it need be no hindrance to pleasant companionship thereon. Throughout his long teaching life this was his characteristic attitude, and his students recognized that his passion for intellectual honesty and hard work were equaled by his kindness and enthusiasm."[8] That passion marked Louise's work throughout her career. She chose to major in Latin because the subject was intellectually demanding and the degree would enable her to support herself as a high school teacher. (A 1900 survey showed that 88 percent of gainfully employed Barnard graduates were teachers.) "I majored in Greek and Latin," she told an interviewer in 1934. "I was preparing to teach, and in those days no one thought of teaching Economics [in high school]. I did, however, take all the Economics I could, as a sort of avocation. I'm just another one of the many cases in which the avocation becomes the vocation."[9]

Barnard and Columbia professors shaped twentieth-century U.S. economic thought and provided scientific tools for the Progressive reform movement. According to Duer Miller, the department emphasized "outstanding economic problems in the light of current facts and of economic analysis ... More and more subjects related to human values and social evolution came into the classroom through this department."[10] Henry L. Moore, who taught the required course on "the characteristics of modern industrial society and the fundamental economic principles," pioneered the use of statistics to extract information about economic policy issues from data—an approach that Louise would apply in her subsequent research. She also took his class on the economic history of England and the United States, which showed the connection between "present economic conditions and the rise of current social problems,"[11] as well as "Theories of Social Reform," taught by John Bates Clark, who was considered the most eminent American economist of his generation. That course must have been a challenge to a student with her limited background in the subject. How would she make sense of his argument that "labor and capital move from separate impulses, since each agent seeks its own interest, and not the interest of the other" but that "their movements are interdependent, since neither of them can move without changing the productive power of the other"?[12] The idea that capital and labor were interdependent stayed with her, however, and informed her efforts as industrial investigator and personnel manager to stress cooperation over confrontation.

During her senior year, Louise deepened her knowledge of the field through a course on "Practical Economics," which covered "money, banking, taxation, government expenditures, foreign trade, monopolies and trusts, and the legal regulation of industry" (in one semester!), and she studied the English Social Reformers with Professor Moore. From him she learned about the Christian Socialists of the mid-nineteenth century and the Fabians, who emphasized society's responsibility for *all* of its members and inspired the foundation of settlement houses in London and, later, the United States. If she remembered the urban scenes she had observed as she was commuting to high school through Harlem's Little Italy, she might have been excited to find explanations of such conditions and learn about people trying to remedy them.

Henry Rogers Seager's course on "The Labor Problem" also inspired Louise. Seager was among the first to introduce the idea of social legislation to protect wage-earners against the impact of illness, unemployment, industrial accidents, and old age. One can imagine how passionate statements like the following would have resonated in the classroom: "Of all the evils that befall the capable and industrious wage earner, none seems so cruel and unjust as unemployment… To have a family dependent on one's earnings, and young children actually in need of food, makes this hardship a bitter wrong. More good men have been transformed into embittered advocates of social revolution by unemployment than by any other single cause." From Professor Seager Louise first heard about the impact of irregular employment, which would become the topic of her master's thesis: "As industry is now organized, there are a large number of occupations which require labor intermittently because the volume of production called for is highly irregular."[13] Some students described his lectures as "a call to battle."[14] Louise would answer that call.

Discovering What Women Could Do

The professors (all male) taught theory, but campus events introduced Louise to women who were applying to real life the principles she studied in class. At a "tea in the Theater" in December 1906, she heard Florence Kelley, a leading figure in the Progressive movement, speak about the campaign to end child labor. Kelley was head of the National Consumers' League, one of several organizations that channeled the civic power of women. Listening to Kelley was exciting: "No other man or woman I have ever heard so blended knowledge of facts, wit, satire, burning indignation, prophetic denunciation—all poured out at white heat in a voice varying from flutelike tones to deep organ tones," wrote her friend and fellow reformer Josephine Goldmark.[15] That evening, Kelley urged her audience of privileged college students to consider that

> We have, in this country, two million children under the age of sixteen years who are earning their bread. They vary in age from six and seven years (in the cotton mills of Georgia) and eight, nine and ten years (in the coal-breakers of Pennsylvania), to fourteen, fifteen and sixteen years in more enlightened states. ... Tonight while we sleep, several thousand little girls will be working in textile mills, all the night through, in the deafening noise of the spindles and the looms spinning and weaving cotton and wool, silks and ribbons for us to buy.[16]

The speech was Louise's introduction to a cause that would engage her later, and one that was high on the agenda of Progressive reformers. The State of New York had passed a law regulating child labor in 1903, and a bill proposing federal rules had been introduced into Congress in 1906. That bill was defeated, but in 1907 Congress chartered the National Child Labor Committee with a board of directors that included Florence Kelley.

Kelley connected the abuses of the system to women's lack of voting rights: "If the mothers and the teachers in Georgia could vote, would the Georgia Legislature have refused at every session for the last three years to stop the work in the mills of children under twelve years of age?" she asked.[17] But, even without the suffrage, women could work for social justice. The Consumers' League operated on the principle that "to live means to buy, to buy means to have power, to have power means to have responsibility." It published "white lists" of shops that met minimum standards of fairness and hygiene and urged boycotts of stores and manufacturers that employed young children and required women to work sixteen hours a day with no pay for overtime.[18]

Two other speakers at the event pointed out ways in which students could join the struggle for social justice. Mary Van Kleeck, director of the Alliance Employment Bureau, which placed women in industrial and clerical jobs, "spoke of her investigation of the working of the sixty-hour law for factory women in New York, of the numerous violations and of the lack of an adequate inspection force."[19] (It is hard now to imagine that limiting women's work to sixty hours a week was an improvement!) Van Kleeck, who had graduated from Smith College only three years earlier, would play a decisive role as mentor, supervisor, and colleague in Louise's future career. Her emphasis on the need for sociological investigation to document abuses and inspire action must have sparked Louise's interest, as would the presentation by Mary Simkhovitch, founder and director of a New York settlement house, who emphasized "the opportunities the Settlement offered to every college woman to share the larger life even though she was not making social work her profession." Her appeal resonated with the audience: "The most gratifying part of the meeting was the interest shown by a number of Barnard students who pledged themselves as workers."[20]

In her course on English social reformers, Louise had heard about settlements like Toynbee Hall in London's East End, a social center for the neighborhood and a residence for the Oxford graduates who worked and *settled* among the poor—hence the term "settlement" for similar institutions established in the United States, like Hull House in Chicago, founded by Jane Addams and Ellen Starr in 1889. Settlement houses met the needs of thousands of workers, mostly immigrants from Southern and Eastern Europe, who were pouring into American cities in response to growing demand for industrial labor. They offered lending libraries, classes in practical skills, lectures on a variety of subjects, meeting space for the discussion of issues, and kindergartens and after-school programs for children. Barnard was a member of the College Settlement Association, which had chapters on several women's college campuses and sponsored a settlement on Rivington Street on Manhattan's Lower East Side.

Events like the ones Louise attended encouraged graduates to become settlement residents, develop a professional interest in social work, and undertake research. The March 21, 1906 issue of the *Barnard Bulletin* announced a fellowship for which seniors could apply: "The object of the fellowship is to open to well-qualified persons the opportunity afforded by Settlement life for investigation of social conditions. ... No requirements are made beyond residence in a Settlement during the academic year and the pursuit of some clearly defined line of work, scientific or practical [which shows] promise of future usefulness." The announcement, which listed her Economics Professor Seager as "referee," must have appealed to Louise. He and her other professors had taught her that the practical application of economic principles could improve the lives of people. Could she make herself useful in this endeavor and turn her avocation into a career? That was a more exciting prospect than becoming a high-school Latin teacher!

Louise had a lot to think about as she rode the streetcar home, sometimes quite late when events kept her on campus, and many ideas and plans to share with her parents, who must have been pleased to watch her benefit from the educational opportunities of their adopted country. Frederikke would have listened with a sympathetic ear to her daughter's growing concern with economic injustice. From her Danish childhood, she recalled the deep poverty of much of the rural population; she wrote a story about "Old Karen," who took care of the pastor's children, mended their clothes, helped with the laundry—and ended her days in the poorhouse.

Tulla had moved to Houston to teach math at her old high school, but the three remaining children contributed to lively conversations around the dinner table, talking about their very different experiences and interests. Fred enrolled as an engineering student at Columbia in 1905 but did not complete his degree although he later worked as an engineer. His passion was automobiles; be bought an old Mercury racing car, which he kept in a lot in the Bronx while storing spare parts under his bed at home. Marguerite took up ice-skating as a high school student, sometimes practicing in Central Park until late at night, and skated professionally for a while. She seems to have had an active social life, judging from her description of her mother, who "always watered her plants in the late evening when I was saying goodbye to my friends on the stoop below. Suddenly my friends would exclaim 'it must be raining' and take off."[21]

The freedom that Gustaf and Frederikke gave their children to develop their talents and choose their own paths in life was remarkable for their time. It included supporting Louise's decision to apply for a fellowship to the College Settlement after graduation. Mary Van Kleeck, who had been a Rivington Street resident after her graduation from Smith College, probably assisted her in developing a proposal to investigate the irregularity of women factory workers' employment, using material available through the Alliance Employment Bureau and the Manhattan Trade School. Clearly, her project met the criterion "promise of future usefulness" because the selection committee awarded her the grant. An October 1907 column in the *Barnard Bulletin* about the activities of recent graduates mentions that Louise Odencrantz "is connected with the Consumers' League and will also do settlement work," so she may have received support from Florence Kelley's organization as well.

While completing a diverse and challenging academic program, which earned her a Phi Beta Kappa key, Louise also engaged in extra-curricular activities. In her senior year, she served as secretary of her class and participated in a performance in Latin of a play by the Roman author Terence, produced by the Classics Club. According to the *Barnard Bulletin*,

> The affair went off very creditably. In particular, praise is due for the good recitation of Latin by the actors in general. They spoke so well that even those spectators who had not had the temerity to continue classical studies after freshman year [when it was mandatory] understood much of what was said. ... The afternoon was a distinct triumph for college spirit. The interest shown by the audience was due to the pride they felt in the new departure as well as to the great amusement furnished by the play itself. Many students remained in the theater till after six o'clock, singing and cheering and making merry over the nectar and ambrosia.

The New York Times carried a notice of the play, which mentioned that "in the flowing robes of the Grecians, Miss Louisa [sic] Odencrantz made a delightful leading lady."[22]

The quote accompanying Louise's photo in the Barnard Yearbook, "What novelty is worth that sweet monotony where everything is known and loved because it is known?" seems an odd choice for somebody about to embrace the new and challenging experience of settlement life. The sentence concludes a passage from George Eliot's *The Mill on the Floss* that begins, "We could never have loved the earth so well if we had had no childhood in it, —if it were not the earth where the same flowers come up again every spring that we used to gather with our tiny fingers as we sat lisping to ourselves on the grass."[23] Was Louise remembering the prairie landscape of her early years and longing for the familiarity and security she had experienced then? Her career would involve "novelty" rather than "monotony," but the consistency of values that drove it and the relationships she developed would give her the sense of belonging for which the George Eliot's character yearns. Unlike the heroine of *The Mill on the Floss*, who died a victim to forces beyond her control, Louise was able to take charge of her own destiny. By the time she walked in the Class Day procession with her fellow Barnard graduates, all wearing white dresses, black academic gowns, and mortarboards, she knew where she was going. She would be a fellow at the College Settlement and take courses in economics and social science at the Columbia Faculty of Political Science, which had accepted her into the master's program.

During the summer after her graduation, Louise stayed at the farm in New Jersey that her parents had bought and where the family spent week-ends and vacations. Sometimes the two Danish cousins, who immigrated to the United States in 1904 and 1907 respectively, joined them. Frederikke seems to have enjoyed returning to rural life now that it was not a struggle for survival as in Nebraska but a leisure activity. The photos that she sent to her relatives in Denmark have a whimsical quality. She staged scenes with titles such as "A real farm family in America," which shows the two young men and Marguerite on top of a hay wagon, Gustaf (dressed in bib overalls) and herself standing in the foreground, all of them holding pitch forks. She captured Marguerite playing with a dog, Fred, tall and handsome, with rolled-up shirt sleeves, holding a cat in his arms, and Louise, perched on a water tank wearing a long light-colored dress with a hemline that has obviously been dragged through the dirt. Looking back, Louise described herself as "gangly—that's what we used to call tall girls when I was young." The photo shows her looking relaxed and confident, but she was about to move into an environment very different from the country setting of her parents' farm.

Louise photographed at her parents' country home in the summer of 1907.

Chapter IV

Fieldwork at the College Settlement

Moving In

During the early 1900s, New York's Lower East Side was the most crowded area in the world. According to the 1910 census, 373,057 people lived in the square-mile area around Rivington Street—a population density five times that of twenty-first century Mumbai. Streets teemed with immigrants recently arrived from Central, Eastern, and Southern Europe; vendors hawked wares from pushcarts—vegetables, fish, pickles, eggs, kitchen utensils, shoes, and other necessities; pedestrians spilled from sidewalks, getting in the way of horse-drawn delivery vehicles; shouts rang out in Yiddish, Russian, and Italian. On hot summer nights, people escaped from the heat and stench of the tenements to breathe the slightly fresher air outside. Photographs show crowds so dense you wonder how one more person could make her way through—like the tall young woman on her way to take up residence at the College Settlement in September 1907.

The high-ceilinged parlors of 95 Rivington Street offered some relief from the crowds and heat outside. The house had been an elegant private home serving as rectory for the German Presbyterian Church, which moved uptown in 1872. The College Settlement Association had acquired the property in 1889 to provide "a home in a neighborhood of working people in which educated women might live" and "furnish a common meeting ground for all classes for their mutual benefit and education."[1] The building was full of activity. The sound of children practicing musical instruments in the basement mingled with the happy noise of kids playing in the

Sunday morning at the corner of Orchard and Rivington Streets. Photo by Bain News Service, N.Y.C. ca. 1910. George Grantham Bain Collection, Prints & Photographs Division, Library of Congress, LC-USZ62-72444.

courtyard behind the house; young women received sewing lessons in the assembly-and-library room, preparing for jobs in the garment industry, while others learned cooking in a fully equipped kitchen. Sometimes, the wide mahogany doors between the two ground-floor rooms opened to create a larger space for meetings and social gatherings. In the afternoon and evening, volunteers taught courses in grammar, reading, dance, Shakespeare, the history of New York City, and other subjects. (One of the instructors at Rivington Street was Eleanor Roosevelt, who taught calisthenics and sometimes invited her fiancé Franklin to accompany her, thus opening his eyes to conditions he had never seen before and laying the foundation for his future commitment to serving the disadvantaged.)

Louise, who had commuted from her parents' home while at Barnard, now had her first experience of living with a group of contemporaries, whose dedication and enthusiasm made settlement houses "exciting, intellectually stimulating places" according to social historian Allen Davis. She spent her days out of the building gathering material for her fellowship project, but at night she returned to share her experiences with the other residents over dinner in the room at the back of the house that served as a dining room when it was not used for classes and meetings. Conversations sometimes continued into the late evening. Throughout the day, the young college graduates followed the advice given to residents at the University Settlement on the corner of Rivington and Eldridge Streets: "Make friends with the tenement people, and listen, listen, listen." In the evening, they processed their impressions of immigrants' struggles with poverty, unemployment, and filthy, crowded living spaces, and reinforced each other's hope that "their books and articles, based upon careful research, [would] document the need for reform and help to convince at least a portion of the American people that social environment, not individual weakness, was the greatest cause of poverty."[2]

Connecting Practice and Theory

The subject of Louise's investigation was the irregular employment of women factory workers. She gathered evidence from visits to workshops on the Lower East Side, mostly small neighborhood establishments that produced clothing, belts, suspenders, hats, cigars, boxes, candy, pencils, etc. Demand for many of these products fluctuated as seasons changed, and so did employment: Straw hat manufacturers closed after three busy months in the spring, and chocolate production slowed down after the Christmas and Easter rushes. Shops hired from a large pool of cheap labor, mostly young and female, ready to carry out tasks that required minimal skills, and hungry for work although the hours were long and the prospects uncertain. At the time when Louise was doing her research, the country was suffering financial unrest, which increased the uncertainty. The stock market panic of October 1907 brought the economy to the brink of collapse, and New York City almost went bankrupt. J.P. Morgan intervened to keep the stock market open and stabilize the situation, but a persistent scarcity of money affected business. Many factories reduced their employees to part-time, and wholesale and resale trades also cut back. As always, the most vulnerable, including the women that Louise investigated, suffered the most.

The Alliance Employment Bureau, directed by Mary Van Kleeck (who guided Louise's research), the Manhattan Trade School, and the Women's Trade Union League made the records of more than 1,100 women available, providing the numerical basis for the study. After collecting the data, Louise processed them in Professor Moore's statistical laboratory at Columbia, which contained "Hollerith tabulating machines, comptometers, and other modern facilities."[3] The tables she produced provide factual evidence of the irregularity of employment. Of the positions reviewed, 68 percent had lasted less than one year, and half of those had ended after less than three months. Another table shows that, during a period of one year, 40 percent of a representative sample group lost between one and three months of work while 21 percent lost even more. Those figures do not include the hours lost by pieceworkers, who were required to show up every morning but would be paid only if and when orders were received. The weekly wage for 48 percent of the women was between $5 and $7 a week; 24 percent earned less, 28 percent more. Given the loss of income due to seasonal unemployment, many women in the middle group earned less than $300 a year—not sufficient for independent living.[4]

The numbers defined the scope and depth of irregular employment, and notes in the records indicated what the causes were. In 55 percent of the cases that Louise examined, the reasons cited for termination of employment were "slack season," "firm failed or moved," or simply "work ended." Some women had been forced to leave because of personal illness or the illness of family members, but "only about ten per cent of the positions were given up because the workers did not like them, because the conditions of work were bad—poor light, dirty work, long hours, night work, etc."[5] Countering the conventional argument that girls, if out of work, could always find something to do at home, Louise emphasized that most of the women she met looked upon themselves mainly as wage earners. They worked because they needed to support themselves or provide income for their family.

What was it like to live with the uncertainty of employment that these women faced? Louise found answers to that question by interviewing working girls in clubs, union offices, or in their own homes in the evening. The conversations opened her mind to the realities of their lives and provided concrete examples for her study. She identified each of the girls that she cited by name, emphasizing their individuality. "Josephine loses two or three months every summer," and "Elsie, a young, capable, energetic girl was laid off from July 4 to September 10." Both of these stayed with the same employer, but Mildred, after being idle about three months, changed jobs and began working overtime until 8 P.M. several days a week without additional compensation. "In slack time ... she sewed for the family, but her mother felt that she could not afford to keep a dressmaker two or three months every year, and was anxious for Mildred to get steady work." Because of terminations, women spent much of their time looking for work. One described a typical day of job-hunting: "I get the papers right away in the morning, but when you come to the place, there are always so many others waiting, and then it is too late to go to any other place. Sometimes the man takes your name and says he will let you know in a couple of days. You wait, but you don't hear a word from him. Half the time he doesn't want anybody. You always feel kind of upset like, and don't feel like doing anything at home."[6]

Louise enjoyed her conversations with these women, entering into their lives and discovering each one's "ways of thinking, her ambitions, her sorrows and worries and her points of happiness," as she told her Barnard classmates.[7] She made friends with many of the young women and gained respect for their courage and persistence and their attempts to make sensible decisions in difficult circumstances. They were a diverse group with different backgrounds. Most were immigrants or the daughters of recent immigrants, who lived in the tenements near Rivington Street, but some came from homes of a better sort; some had special training for the work they entered, others had none. All of them faced the same uncertain employment conditions, which underscored the idea that social and economic circumstances, rather than individual qualities, determined the outcome.

The goal of the Manhattan Trade School for Girls, which opened in 1902 and from whose records Louise drew much of her material, was to train "the youngest and poorest wage-earners to be self-supporting as quickly as possible," providing them with skills in particular trades (millinery, hand-sewing, dress-making, machine operating etc.) as well as knowledge of arithmetic, English, history, geography, civics, and "the ability to grasp the important factors in any situation and then go to work without waste of time or motion"[8] —a life skill that Louise would apply in her future positions. Unfortunately, she found, girls that had received such education were as likely to lose their jobs in slack seasons as were those without training, so many of them abandoned the trade they had studied to enter another that promised steady work. She cited the example of Elizabeth and her sister, who, although trained as dressmakers, had given up that line of work because it left them unemployed three or four months every year and instead supported their widowed mother by working year-round as telephone operators.

The Trade School offered programs training students in the use of the technical equipment that was making much manual labor redundant, hoping by "awakening intelligent interest in the ... machine, to kindle ambition in the workers" and aiming "to put a thinker behind every machine as its operator."[9] Indeed, machine operating was well paid and less likely to suffer from slack seasons, but, Louise noted, "it requires close and strained watching of the needle, it is extremely noisy. It is very confining, and a girl is often forced to sit in the same position throughout the day." Several girls she interviewed had left such jobs on account of ill health, including one who found more wholesome work in a cigar factory. Although the reality of machine operating might not match expectations, Louise recognized the importance of the school not only "training girls for better and more lucrative work" but giving them "a better understanding of the worth of their labor and the means of securing a just return for it."[10]

The Columbia Catalog cautioned that "in those subjects in which field-work is required for a satisfactory essay, the candidate is advised to perform it before entering the University,"[11] but Louise combined graduate courses, research, and settlement residence. It only took her thirty minutes to travel from the lower East Side to Morningside Heights on the newly opened IRT subway line from

City Hall to uptown Manhattan, but the cultural and psychological distance between the two worlds was huge. Linking the two contexts was, however, the essence of her experience: she would apply the theoretical knowledge she gained at Columbia to the reality of Rivington Street, which in turn would inform her understanding of the theory. Fortunately, the course requirements for the M.A. degree were flexible ("The number of courses and in general the amount of work to be taken in each subject is determined, for each student, by the professor or professors in charge of the [major] subject"),[12] and the department gave her credit for three economics courses she had completed as an undergraduate.

Louise took a seminar in Political Economy and Finance. Recalling that experience a few years later, she described herself as "one of two lone women in the Columbia Economics Seminar of some fifty Japs [sic!], Americans, Chinese, Russians and other miscellanies. If my mind had not been so full of the unemployment of factory girls, the seminar would have offered a good thesis on the immigrant question."[13] Another course related more closely to her settlement residency: "Social Economics: Poverty and Relief," taught by Edward Thomas Devine, who, while trained as an economist, had a major influence on the emerging profession of social work. He urged social workers to "seek out and strike effectively at those organized forces of evil, at those particular causes of dependence and intolerable living conditions which are beyond the control of individuals whom they injure and whom they too often destroy."[14] She also found time to study the history of Great Britain during the eighteenth and nineteenth centuries with Professor Herbert Osgood, who stressed the interaction between political institutions and economic forces. Somehow, she managed to complete the courses and submit her thesis by the April 15th deadline. It met Columbia's criteria ("it is expected that the master's essay shall be something more than a restatement of things well done"),[15] and, in June, she received her master's degree in social science.

The Rivington Street experience and the coursework for the degree became the foundation of Louise's future career. She developed the mindset that Allen Davis finds characteristic of settlement workers, "an idealistic faith in the future [combined] with a hard-headed realism about how change is accomplished in a democracy,"[16] and she learned that, although she did not have the right to vote, she could help bring about change through research and advocacy. Like other educated middle-class women who joined the settlement movement, she was, in the words of historian Domenica Barbuto, "given a chance to move beyond the traditional confines of the home and to enter the working world in positions of leadership, achieving a level of equality with their male colleagues."[17] When the fellowship ended, Mary Van Kleeck hired her as statistician and investigator for the Committee on Women's Work, a small independent research organization, affiliated with the Alliance Bureau of Employment and the Manhattan Trade School. Professor Seager, who had introduced Louise to the subject of irregular employment and directed her thesis, served as chair of the committee's board and probably supported her appointment. It was a modest beginning, but it took her beyond the teaching profession, another "traditional confine" of female employment, for which her undergraduate degree in Latin had prepared her.

A Significant First Publication

The settlement experience led to the publication of Louise's first article, derived from her master's thesis, in the May 1909 issue of *The Survey*, a national journal that published the work of leading social scientists and reformers. Photos by Lewis Hine enhanced the impact of the article. Hine, one of the major documentary photographers of the century, was working for the National Child Labor Committee at the time, producing images of children working in cotton mills, mines, canneries, and factories. A study of Hine's technique emphasizes his "strong and passionate desire to humanize his subjects – to make them appear as real as they would if one was really standing there" and to extract "individuals with little financial import from obscurity." That intention is evident in the photos accompanying the *Survey* article.[18] The tie-in between text and illustrations suggests that he and Louise worked together, walking the streets of the Lower East Side studying the conditions of their subjects.

Considering the cumbersome equipment that the photographer used and the time he would need to set it up, the spontaneous quality of the photos is striking. One features two women sitting on benches in Union Square early in the morning; one is scanning a newspaper intently for openings; the other looks as if she has given up hope. In another photo, clusters of people are waiting outside two workshops; the women, dressed in jackets, long pleated skirts, and big hats with flowers and feathers, appear to be talking to each other; the men stand a little apart, as if they are embarrassed to queue up for work. A third picture shows the futility of job hunting: A woman is standing at the foot of a staircase leading to a shop, glowering at the closed door, her mouth open in an exclamation of disappointment; next to the stairs, a child is crouching in front of a cat, indicating that the neighborhood is residential as well as commercial; off to the side, a man is loading a box onto a horse-drawn cart. (What was it like to cross the street wearing a long skirt in a city served by 120,000 horses, each one producing thirty pounds of manure a day?) Other photos show hand-written signs announcing jobs for "sleeve-makers," "fancy feather hands," "feather curlers," "copyists on hats," "sewers and small girls" (the latter were cheaper). Workers were needed at the time, but not for long.

At the age of twenty-four, Louise joined a distinguished list of authors promoting social justice in the pages of *The Survey*. Events during the following year would focus New York's attention on problems of women factory workers like the ones she had described, and as a member of the Committee on Women's Work—soon to become part of the Russell Sage Foundation—she would continue efforts to change those conditions. The curiosity that led her to study economics and immerse herself in the life of the Lower East Side, her empathy with the women she interviewed, and her ability to tell their stories had defined her career path and aligned it with the reform movement of the early twentieth century.

Chapter V

Increased Attention to Women Workers

Industrial Unrest

The summer after the publication of Louise's article was a period of significant unrest in New York's garment industry. In July 2009, 200 women walked out of the Rosen Brothers Shirtwaist Factory in protest against a reduction in the piecework rate. Shirtwaist blouses were a high-demand fashion item that appealed to women of all classes; female workers in Lewis Hine's photos wore them, and so did Barnard undergraduates. Like several other companies, Rosen Brothers rented a large factory loft with space for power-driven machinery that increased efficiency and with better light and more air than the small workshops Louise had studied. To keep costs low, however, owners maintained tight control over workers, required them to work sixty hours a week or more during the busy season (without overtime pay), charged them for electricity and thread used in sewing, and found other ways of reducing wages.

After a five-week strike, the Rosen employees got a ten-percent wage increase and returned to work. Their success inspired strikes at other companies, which hired strikebreakers to continue production, as well as "security guards" (prize-fighters and ex-convicts) to "protect" them when they crossed the picket lines and to beat up strike-leaders. Among the latter was nineteen-year-old Clara Lemlich, who was left bleeding on the sidewalk of 17th Street north of Union Square with six broken ribs. Police arrested more than 700 of the strikers, and the courts, siding with the owners, handed down fines and prison sentences to the women while letting the "guards" go free.

On November 22, Lemlich, who had recovered from her injuries after several weeks in a hospital, gave a rousing speech to a meeting of shirtwaist workers in Cooper Union's Great Hall of the People. The next day, thousands joined the strike, which has become known as the "Uprising of 20,000" but actually involved twice that many women, who were tired of low wages, reduced by deductions for supplies and mistakes, long hours, and dehumanizing treatment by employers: They had to eat meals at their sewing machines, their bathroom breaks were closely monitored, and they were searched when they left work because of the suspicion of theft. Employers, again supported by the police, responded by hiring scabs to continue production and thugs to beat up picketers.

Reports of police brutality inspired middle- and upper-class women to join the picket lines, and the arrest of one of them, Mary Dreier, head of New York Women's Trade Union League, made front-page headlines. When Progressive reformers like Professor Seligman of Columbia and settlement leaders Mary Simkhovich and Lillian Wald wrote to the *New York Times* in protest, the paper defended the police insisting they were just doing their duty, but the exchange raised public awareness and influenced opinion. Gradually, individual companies settled, agreeing to a 52-hour work week, increased pay, and—in some cases—recognition of the International Ladies Garment Workers Union. In February 1910, the strike was called off. Working conditions remained hazardous, however, especially at the Triangle Shirtwaist Company, which did not accept all the terms but offered enough of a pay raise to persuade workers to return.[1]

The Russell Sage Foundation Embraces Women's Issues

The strike brought increased attention to the treatment of women in factories and contributed to the decision by the Russell Sage Foundation Board to bring the Committee on Women's Work in-house as a permanent department with offices at 31 Union Square. Founded in 1907 by Margaret Sage (1828–1918) with a $10 million gift from the estate of her deceased husband, the Russell Sage Foundation defined its goal as "the improvement of social and living conditions in the United States of America." Russell

Sage, a robber baron of the Gilded Age, who opposed any kind of philanthropy, had built a fortune investing in railroads and lumber; after his death, his widow found great satisfaction in using his fortune to do good works. She told the first meeting of the board of trustees, which she chaired for several years, "I am nearly eighty years old, and I feel as if I were just beginning to live."[2] The original board had four other female members, and the Foundation hired women experts to head departments and conduct investigations. Its first major project was the *Pittsburgh Survey*, a comprehensive sociological study of working and living conditions in the city of Pittsburgh.

Historians describe the Russell Sage Foundation as "a think tank for the Progressive Era" and "a national center for the study of social welfare policy and for the promotion of cooperation among charity societies and related organizations," which united in its initial program "two complementary efforts: to professionalize social work and to eliminate deleterious environmental conditions." To achieve its objectives, the Foundation assembled "perhaps the best group of empirical social researchers in the nation."[3] Incorporating the Committee on Women's Work, whose research it had been funding for several years, was part of this purpose according to John M. Glenn, director of the Foundation during its first 24 years: "In view of the value of the facts that had been gathered … it seemed important to round out the investigations and still more important not to lose from our staff such good investigators."[4]

Professor Seager remained as chair of the Committee on Women's Work, providing a link with Columbia University, and Mary Van Kleeck continued to supervise the unit's activities, assisted by Louise and other staff that joined her at the Union Square Office. Young as they were (Van Kleeck was twenty-seven at the time), the group had the experience, energy, and dedication to carry out the ambitious agenda set by the board: Continue the investigations of the bookbinding trade and the millinery industry that the Manhattan Trade School had requested and initiate two new studies, one of artificial flower-making and another of working girls in evening schools. They carried out research in all four areas simultaneously between 1910 and 1912 with work on millinery and evening schools continuing into 1913.

Louise, who prepared the statistical tables for the four studies and took part in the field work, enjoyed charting new territory, as she told an interviewer from the *Barnard College Alumnae Monthly* in 1935: "These were practically the first industrial studies made, very elementary of course, but there was no place to go for precedent as to method; it was great fun sheer pioneering."[5] She and her colleagues were in fact developing the method of feminist research, which, according to Sandra Harding, "begins with women's experience as the basis for social analysis," aims to benefit women, and assumes that "the researcher is not a neutral observer but is on the same critical plane as the subject matter."[6]

Affiliation with the Russell Sage Foundation expanded the scope of the original investigations to include issues that all women factory workers faced. Bookbinding, which employed 6,000 women in New York City alone, provided an example of current efforts to speed up industrial production through mechanization and the specialization of functions. The study aimed to show the impact of this trend on workers and the risks to which it exposed them but also to suggest how all stakeholders could work together to improve conditions for the benefit of everybody. In the introduction to *Women in the Bookbinding Trade,* published in 1913, Van Kleeck proposed "to discover the constructive forces potent in the industry, to disclose opportunities for further improvements by employers, workers, and the community." Such an analysis "should point the way toward changing the lot of women in many industries in which similar conditions exist."[7]

The introduction also outlined the approach of the study: "Observe shop conditions at first hand, interview employers, and [get] to know a number of … women personally in their own homes."[8] In order to identify workplaces that would adequately represent the entire trade, the investigators visited 417 workshops engaged in "binding" a wide range of paper products including individual volumes for private customers, trade books for publishers, telephone directories, magazines, pamphlets, and theater programs. Conditions in the shops, most of them located in the area around City Hall east of Broadway, varied significantly. Some occupied large lofts of high buildings with good lighting and ventilation, accessible by "modern passenger elevators," but others were dark, stuffy, and overcrowded. The researchers noted the irony of girls "stitching a magazine 'devoted to the interests of health,' in a cellar workroom entirely below street level, lighted by gas" and found that "the lack of proper ventilation endangers the workers' health in too many binderies. Books piled high cut off light and air." Walking up and down "long flights of dark and dusty wooden stairs" or using slow freight "hoists" with warning signs ("All persons riding in this elevator do so at their own risk"), they must have wondered what would happen in an emergency.[9]

The Triangle Fire Rouses Public Attention

While Louise and her colleagues were gathering data, a disaster occurred that shocked the public and did more to raise awareness of factory conditions than the combined efforts of the National Consumers' League and the Russell Sage Foundation: the Triangle Shirtwaist Factory fire. On March 26, 1911, the headline of *The New York Times'* front page was "Men and Girls Die in Waist Factory Fire; Trapped high up in Washington Place Building; Street Strewn with Bodies; Piles of Dead inside." Beneath the headline was a photo of the Asch Building with a fire-truck ladder reaching only the sixth of ten floors; the Triangle Factory occupied the top three levels. The timing of the fire added to the pathos: It began at 4:40 P.M. on Saturday afternoon, nearly five hours after the employees in the rest of the building had been allowed to go home. The owners kept doors locked to prevent staff from sneaking outside for breaks or carrying off merchandise. As a result, when the fire broke out, igniting the fabric scraps that littered the crowded workrooms, the employees faced a choice between dying of burns and smoke inhalations inside or jumping to an instant death on the sidewalk. Only a few survived by climbing stairs to the roof, where New York University students attending a class next door rescued them.

Of the 146 victims, 123 were immigrant girls in their late teens and early twenties, who could barely speak English, and "almost all were the main support of their hard-working families."[10] Frances Perkins, who had been investigating working conditions for the National Consumers League, was attending a social function in Greenwich Village when the fire broke out and rushed to the site in time to see women's bodies flying through the air and crashing on the pavement. According to her biographer Kirstin Downey, that moment "was the first time she recognized that tragedies could be turned into positive events. She realized it might be possible to capitalize on the outrage the city felt to get substantive reforms made".[11] In response to the lobbying efforts of Perkins and others, the New York State Legislature created the Factory Investigating Commission and charged it with examining industrial conditions and recommending necessary changes.

Women in the Bookbinding Trade

Louise and her colleagues completed the fieldwork for the bookbinding study in July 1911. Women employed in this trade differed from the garment workers that perished in the Triangle fire in one respect: 90 percent of them were born in the United States; 29 percent had native-born parents, and the largest group (36 percent) were children of Irish fathers, "a nationality not regarded as 'foreign' in New York." Thus, the study implied, recent immigrants were not the only victims of ruthless employers: "the book-binding trade in New York is an excellent occupation in which to study the conditions of employment of native born, wage-earning women."[12]

The researchers interviewed individual women to discover the impact on their lives of conditions at work. In the course of the study, they made a total of 732 visits to 362 women's homes, securing 201 complete records from sources "varied enough to inspire confidence in the representative character of the results." Van Kleeck insisted the investigators conduct no more than two home visits in an evening in order to allow "plenty of time ... for full and frank discussion." She also instructed them not to take notes during the interviews because that might have "a chilling effect" but to fill in cards with pre-printed questions and room for details as soon as possible afterwards in order not to miss any of the specifics that would add authenticity to their account.[13]

After long evenings talking to women in their homes, the investigators met to write down the information they had collected, compare notes, and process their impressions together. Their methodology illustrates Cynthia Enloe's definition of feminist research in *The Curious Feminist*: "One of the starting points of feminism is taking women's lives seriously. 'Seriously' implies listening carefully, digging deep, developing a long attention span, being ready to be surprised." She describes the female investigator as being "still wide awake and curious when the meeting-after-the-meeting continues among a select few down the corridor and into the pub."[14] Louise and her colleagues did not go to the pub, but the sharing of information became an integral part of their method.

The investigators completed thousands of cards. The quotes that appear in the published studies add color to the factual information provided and enhance the reader's sense of the subjects' humanity. One woman, who had spent the day carrying materials to work stations and returning finished products to storage rooms sighed, "I was so tired at night I could hardly keep my eyes open at supper; I wish I had some of those things you put on your feet to measure the distance you walk; I'd like to know how many miles I walk in a day. ... The folding machines are at the other end of the bindery, and we carry the work the distance from one street to another. That's a block."[15]

Others complained that, even if they wore gloves or bandages, their hands and wrists swelled from hours of repetitive movements such as inserting the large sheets of a magazine one within another. One seventeen-year-old said that tending four folding machines made her so nervous she frequently cried from fatigue when she reached home at night. Another young woman complained of severe pain in her left side from weeks spent pressing the foot-pedal on a machine punching holes in notebooks: "Katie looks worn out and is discouraged because she doesn't get more than $7.00 [a week] for the hard work she is doing. She was busy washing the supper dishes at 8.20 P.M. Her younger sister was dressing to go to a wedding. Katie said that she used to go to dances and weddings when she was young, but she is too tired to go now; she is twenty-two years old."[16] Louise's concern for this girl caused her to step outside her investigator role; in her notes to Barnard classmates, she mentioned "getting a place in the country for Katie, an Irish bookbinder, pale and worn out."[17]

Some statements might have made Louise and the other college-educated investigators smile. The binders were responsible for positioning frontispiece illustrations opposite title pages, and sometimes they made mistakes. One girl had pasted "a picture of Longfellow in a copy of *As You Like It*. Nobody knew it until she looked at another girl's book that had a picture of Shakespeare. She said, 'That doesn't look like the picture I pasted. He was a funny looking man, but not as funny as that.'"[18]

Most of the issues mentioned were of a more serious nature. The introduction of machines caused many complaints: "You never know when you'll be laid off. The machines are driving the girls out." When women learned to use the machines, they faced the risk of accidents, for which they received no compensation: "If you lose your finger the boss ain't goin' to do anything for you. I've seen girls get the ends of their fingers cut off by the machine," one complained. The feeder of a folding machine demonstrated how she had to put her hands under the knife and draw them back before the knife came down. "We work on machines at our own risk," she said. Fatigue induced by long working hours during busy seasons increased accidents. A sixteen-year-old girl "wire-stitched her finger one Sunday morning early when she had been working steadily since Saturday at 8.30 A.M." in a magazine bindery.[19]

Details such as these documented the impact of the data on working hours that Louise processed. The State of New York restricted women's work to sixty hours a week and a maximum of twelve hours each day, but employers found ways of circumventing the law during busy seasons by having girls work until midnight on one day and starting a new working day when the date changed at 12 A.M., thus clocking twenty-four successive hours. The law that made it illegal for women under twenty-one to work after 9 P.M. was frequently violated; a seventeen-year-old girl, who stitched programs for opera houses and theaters, worked more than fourteen hours a day during the season and walked home alone from a plant near the Bowery at midnight, risking her safety: "Only bums are down there at that hour of the night," she said.[20]

Louise's statistical charts also illustrated the issue of wages. The median income for all women was $300 a year; for women over twenty-one, it was $400. Irregularity of employment reduced wages as did fines and fees like those that the striking shirtwaist workers had complained about. Some shops charged five cents every two weeks for ice water in summer and two cents a month for having the toilets cleaned (although girls had to bring their own towels and soap). Women's average weekly wages were exactly half those of male workers. The study argued against the prevailing assumption that girls did not need to earn as much as men because they lived at home and were merely supplementing family income. Actually, the financial contribution of daughters was essential; in more than a third of the households visited, mothers had to earn money by factory work or paid work at home, and the fact that they were underpaid was "a prime cause of poverty, preventing wholesome and decent living in thousands of families which depend wholly or in part upon women's earnings."[21]

The conclusion of the study expressed confidence that scientific evidence about the impact of low wages and injurious working conditions would inspire new legislation. The fact that "a new political party" (Theodore Roosevelt's Progressive Party), had adopted such standards as part of its platform suggested that this was an issue that had wide popular appeal. Jane Addams, who had seconded Theodore Roosevelt's nomination at the 1912 convention, wrote the section of the platform on social and industrial justice, which included minimum wage standards, the elimination of child labor, and the prohibition of night work for women and emphasized the need for further study to guide implementation of these principles.[22]

Research on Milliners' Wages Inspires Reform Efforts

The New York State Legislature recognized that wages were an important issue. In 1913, it authorized the Factory Investigation Commission, which had initially focused on fire hazards and sanitation, to study wages and devise methods of ensuring that they allowed workers to maintain a reasonable standard of living. In pursuit of this goal, the Commission enlisted the cooperation of the Russell Sage Foundation, which added the review of wage records to its ongoing investigation of the millinery industry. In 1908, the Manhattan Trade School had requested a study of what was, at the beginning of the twentieth century, one of the largest industrial employers of women. About 134,000 women throughout the United

States were engaged in producing the huge broad-brimmed hats decorated with feathers and artificial flowers that were fashionable at the time. Even the job-seeking women illustrating Louise's *Survey* article wore elaborate flower- and feather-trimmed head gear. Millinery was, however, a seasonal occupation, and thus "study of it should illuminate the whole problem of unemployment and irregular work"—the subject that Louise had researched for her master's thesis.[23]

The title of the published report, *A Seasonal Industry*, reflects that emphasis. The initial approach of the millinery investigation was the same as that used in other studies: factory visits and interviews with individual workers at home. The businesses examined were located all over New York City. They included "large and fashionable establishments of Fifth Avenue" as well as "small shops on Third Avenue, big supply houses on lower Broadway" and "the typical Division Street retail shop with its unique method of soliciting customers by stationing on the sidewalk a 'puller-in,' a stalwart woman who seizes passersby and drags them into the store, there to be dealt with by an equally importunate saleswoman."[24]

When the investigators expanded research to include wage records, they found employers reluctant to release the data requested. One female owner of a millinery shop "objected to the investigation because it would make her employees feel too independent and would give them a notion that their wages should be higher ... If a girl 'does not like her pay in one shop, she can go to another.'" A manager told a researcher who was copying payrolls "in whatever corner of office or workroom happened to be unoccupied" that "it's an awful bother having you here. You're in our way."[25] The investigators persisted, however, because the analysis of payrolls provided the documentation needed to bring about change: "Nothing socially disastrous is inevitable. Such faith, however, if it is to be fulfilled, must be particularized," Van Kleeck argued. "An inadequate wage and irregular employment keep the workers constantly near the margin where going into debt or obtaining assistance from others becomes necessary." Because thousands of women and minors received too low a wage to maintain them in health and decent comfort, "the State is justified in protecting the under-paid women workers and minors in the interest of the State and society."[26] The Commission supported that conclusion and introduced a bill calling for voluntary compliance with minimum wage recommendations, but it did not pass.

Other forms of collaboration with the New York network of social reformers also increased during the years after the Triangle fire. In a letter to Foundation director John Glenn, Van Kleeck mentioned that Josephine Goldmark, was "very anxious to know when our millinery material will be available as the Ohio case concerning a millinery establishment has been appealed to the Supreme Court."[27] Goldmark, Florence Kelley's chief assistant at the National Consumers League, was gathering evidence for her brother-in-law Louis Brandeis to use in his pro bono defense of laws upholding the rights of workers. In 1908, when he defended an Oregon law before the Supreme Court which made it illegal for women to work more than ten hours a day in factories and laundries, she had prepared the first so-called "Brandeis brief" for him, which provided scientific evidence showing the human impact of the law. In a unanimous decision, the Supreme Court had upheld the Oregon law.

In 1908, Goldmark had relied on European sources because no documentation of conditions in the United States was available, but, when a similar case was brought before the Supreme Court a few years later, she provided evidence from Russell Sage Foundation research done in New York City. The following year, when Brandeis argued before the New York Court of Appeals in favor of a law that prohibited employment of women in all factories of the state between 10 P.M. and 6 A.M., Goldmark provided him with evidence from the New York State Factory Investigation Committee and from the statistics that Louise had produced for *Women in the Bookbinding Trade*. This information supported the need for legal restrictions on night work and on the length of the work day in order to avoid situations in which "a ten-hour day on Tuesday could legally be joined at midnight to a ten-hour day on Wednesday."[28] The Court reversed its earlier decision "in the light of all the facts and arguments now presented to us ... because they have been developed by study and investigation."[29]

The court decisions vindicated the idea of the Russell Sage Foundation that "careful, scientific investigation" such as that practiced by its own researchers and the Factory Investigating Commission, could be "a contribution toward the forming of the new social mind ... which shall get things done through the force of opinion."[30] The conclusion of the book-binding study states the same fundamental principle of Progressive reform:

> The interest of the community should make possible a just balance between the demands of worker and employer. The worker aims to secure higher wages to make possible a better standard of living. The employer is anxious to keep down expenses. The public interest would combine and balance these two views, pointing out that production cheapened at the expense of decent living conditions for the workers in reality costs too much. Without such a balance as the community alone can give, there is too often blind conflict of interests of a just and reasonable adoption of proper standards. Public attention is the vital factor needed to focus attention on conditions of employment and to establish throughout the trade the standards which are essential to the health and happiness of thousands of working girls. The task is large and complex, but it is also an encouraging one.[31]

Artificial Flowers: Tenement Home Work and Child Labor

The expansion of the research to include wages delayed the publication of the millinery study until 1917, but, in the meantime, the Committee on Women's Work completed a related investigation of the making of artificial flowers, which were used not only for the trimming of hats but for decoration in middle-and upper-class homes at a time when fresh flowers were not readily available. Three-fourths of all production took place in New York City, "congested in the small and flowerless district south of 14th Street, west of Broadway."[32] Artificial flower-making was primarily handiwork, requiring only limited skills and equipment, and much of the work could be done at home by families, including young children. Thus, a study of the trade exposed several problems: seasonal work, child labor, and "sweated" work done in tenements. As in the other studies, the focus was on "the wellbeing of the girls employed, in-

Original photo text: "Mortaria family, 8 Downing St., N.Y., making flowers wreaths. The little three-year-old on left was actually helping, putting the center of the flower into the petal, and the family said she often works irregularly until 8:00 P.M. The other children, 9, 11, and 14 yrs. old work much later (until 10:00 P.M.)" Photo by Lewis Hine in National Child Labor Committee Collection, Prints & Photographs Division, Library of Congress, LC-USZ62-45843.

sofar as it could be measured in wages, hours of labor, regularity of employment, opportunity to acquire skill, chance to advance, and the conditions of living made possible by the earnings received."[33]

Louise produced thirty-six statistical tables documenting these indicators, but her most significant contribution was her vivid account of encounters with individual women during the field investigation. She spent an evening at the home of seventeen-year-old Theresa Albino on Thompson Street in what is now known as Soho and was then an Italian neighborhood. Theresa, who had started making flowers when she was five years old and left school at fourteen to take a job in a shop nearby, shared the "old, ramshackle and dirty" apartment with her parents, three brothers, and three younger sisters. Everybody made flowers except the father, who earned $1.25 a day pumping water, and an older son employed as a wagon boy.

An appendix to the book reproduced the cards that Louise completed after her visit. She observed that "the mother works by day with the help of the children who are too young to go to school. The school children work after three and in the evening, when Theresa also helps. On the evening of the visit, the family sat down to work immediately after supper. The three-year old worked as steadily as any of the others." The family complained that Annie, aged four, "is lazy and wants to play so that she makes less than Lizzie," the three-year-old. Theresa told Louise that her "mother works all the time—all day, Sundays and holidays, except when she is cooking or washing. She never has time to go out or she would get behind in her work." Theresa herself contributed as well as she could, but she never earned more than $5 a week. "It is awful to work so hard and not to get more pay," she said, and she felt she had to take part in the flower-making at home although "she found the night work very tiring."[34]

Louise obviously sympathized with Theresa, who "is very pale, with black rings about her eyes and looks very tired," and tried to counsel her. Could she look for another job after the slack season? How about improving her prospects by taking classes? She mentioned that she had often thought of going to evening school, but "when it gets busy in the trade, we have to take work home, and I knew I would have to stop then, so what was the use of starting?" Unlike many Italians, Theresa responded enthusiastically to the question about whether it would be a good idea to have a flower-makers' union, "Gee! Wouldn't it! They have a union in sewing and look how much money they get. But ours is a scab place." The impressions Louise collected from this and other interviews stayed with her, inspiring her commitment to ending child labor and supporting young people in their search for training and jobs.[35]

Working Girls in Evening Schools

Many of the public evening schools investigated by the Russell Sage Foundation study were located on the Lower East Side, beyond the Bowery, where "the streets at night are ablaze with light and gay with activity... open shops line the way; noisy voices of push-cart peddlers cry their wares; and men, women and babies crowd the sidewalk."[36] That neighborhood was familiar to Louise from her residency at the settlement on Rivington Street, but the new project brought her into contact with a different group of women than those she had interviewed then. Half of them were Jewish girls from Russia, or Austria-Hungary, or Germany; some were the daughters of parents who had immigrated before or after they were born; others had arrived on their own. The principal of a high school for working women on the corner of Hester and Exeter Streets "told of the inspiration she had gained from the thoughtful and earnest foreign girls who came to classes there ... eager to learn all they could about America; keen and independent in judgment; and withal, ready to make sacrifices not for themselves alone but for their fellow-workers, to improve the conditions in their trades." Many had been involved in the 1910 shirtwaist-workers' strike, "but no less important cause could keep them away from class any night in the term."[37]

Personal interviews with individual women were a significant part of the research for this as for the other projects; in some cases, the same contacts provided answers for more than one study, and occasionally the conversation turned to topics beyond the assigned questions, suggesting that investigator and subject had become friends. For example, Louise talked with a young Russian woman about "socialism, women's rights, trade unions, Bernard Shaw, the drama in America, the school system, and Russian versus American women." The speaker was disappointed in the latter: "They don't care about anything but making dates. It's all men and dances, and they don't care about organizing because they expect to get married and stop working. It's no use talking to them. When you begin on unions, they call you a Socialist, and that ends it; or if you talk about women's suffrage, they laugh at you. Why should they laugh? ... They don't think—but then not many people do in any country. American women are not disturbed enough. You have to be disturbed to think."[38]

Louise undoubtedly enjoyed talking with this articulate and opinionated woman, but she got along equally well with members of other groups, especially the Italians, whose daughters made up only 3.8 percent of the students. She admired the willingness of these girls to challenge the norms of their culture: "The Italians who find their way into evening schools are those who have acquired a point of view quite different from their nation. For an Italian girl to be away from home at night unattended is to oppose custom and run the risk of unpleasant gossip in the neighborhood, even though she does not thereby incur the disapproval of her family ... The object of Italian parents is to marry their daughters well and young." Evidently, the women interviewed were comfortable enough with Louise to ask about her personal life, as suggested by the following passage from the published study: "Many a time has one of our investigators been met with the kindly and courteous, but pitying, comments of Italian men and women who have marveled at her cheerfulness though still unmarried after the ripe age of twenty-five." In her notes to Barnard classmates, Louise gave a pithy version of such a conversation: "One married shirtwaist maker asked me the other night, 'You got a fellow?' and when I replied 'No,' she exclaimed, 'What's the matter?'"[39]

Louise and her colleagues admired the courage and talents of bright and ambitious women, like the Hungarian girl who had come to the United States on her own at the age of seventeen, spoke six languages, and had trained both as a dressmaker and a bookkeeper. "The gift and determination of this girl to advance would be inspiring were not one disheartened by the realization of how little use the industrial world had made of her talents."[40] They were also concerned, however, about the many girls toiling at tasks that required no special training—like the one "whose sole occupation was to put nuts on cakes and whose previous work had been to paste chenille dots on veils"—and emphasized that, besides imparting specific skills, schools had a responsibility to "broaden the outlook" of these workers.[41]

Louise and the other investigators had benefited from a college education and the opportunity to enter new professional fields, but they wanted the public to recognize that girls who had not had those advantages were already contributing to society and could do much more if given the chance: "The fact that women have been tried and not found wanting in so great a variety of occupations indicates that we have in them a great potential force for the material service of humanity, if only we can so change conditions as to give free play to that force." To the authors of the study, that transformation was a matter of common sense. More than a hundred years after the publication of *Working Girls in Evening Schools*, some would argue, the vision of the young researchers is still a work in progress. [42]

Chapter VI

Gaining Professional Recognition

Beyond Statistics

Statistics were an important item in Louise's job description although she had no formal training in the subject. Describing her recent activities to Barnard classmates in 1912, she lamented, "Why didn't I take a course in Statistics instead of Art Appreciation? It would have saved me many a worry. For the last months I have been playing statistician and I feel as if my legs were tables, my arms appendices, my body a census volume, covered with dollar marks and percents and diagrams. Even in writing this I can scarcely refrain from inserting a few tables and statistics."[1] She tabulated data for the four Russell Sage studies in which she participated, including twenty-eight tables, graphs, pie charts, and supplementary pages of figures for *Working Girls in Evening Schools.* In the introduction to that book, Van Kleeck mentioned that the statistical work was done "under the direction of Miss Odencrantz," suggesting that the latter had some assistance. Her May 1912 letter to Director John Glenn reported that "Dr. Ayres and Mr. Clark have gone over the statistics in [the] reports and have had a conference with Miss Odencrantz."[2] Leonard Ayres became head of the Department of Statistics that the Foundation created later that year, and Earle Clark served on his staff; Ayres developed standards of graphic representation for the American Statistical Association and served as statistician for the U.S. Army during both world wars. The conference cited suggests that the two professionals approached Louise as a colleague and respected her contribution.

The Committee on Women's Work also relied on Louise's

judgement in other ways. In the same letter to John Glenn, Van Kleeck mentioned that she had rejected a New York State Department of Labor challenge to a Foundation exposé of unsanitary conditions in a candy factory because "Miss Odencrantz who interviewed the worker feels thoroughly convinced that the girl's complaint was correct."[3] Clearly, Louise's opinion carried weight, which was probably also the reason why her boss dispatched her to Washington with a colleague "during their spring vacations" to inspect the Government Printing Office near Union Station and the Bureau of Engraving and Printing, then housed in building on 14th Street and Independence Avenue, which is now part of the Department of Agriculture.

Although this was Louise's first visit to the nation's capital, she and her colleague did not have much time to explore the sights since they had to visit the two establishments during the daytime as well as at night. They found Uncle Sam's employment practices no better than those in private factories. Women, most of whom were middle-aged, had to stand in front of machines throughout their working hours, they reported, but "the most objectionable feature in the Government Printing Offices is the shifts of workers." Three of the shifts—4 PM to 12.30 A.M., 7 P.M. to 3:30 A.M., and midnight to 8 A.M.—required night-time commuting, and "Washington people who know the girls employed here speak of the danger of their going home alone so late and also of the fact that there is no time between shifts for the airing of the workrooms."[4]

Most significantly for Louise's career, Van Kleeck proposed putting her in charge of a new project, an investigation of Italian women and girls in industry, which had begun in December 1911. In May 1912, Van Kleeck wrote to John Glenn about this project: "I should like to have Miss Odencrantz take charge definitely of the field work and the statistical work attending to the details of watching investigators' reports, etc. She is exceedingly well equipped for such a position, and I think that to organize our work in this way would greatly increase our efficiency." Leading this investigation meant a significant promotion for Louise, who had just turned twenty-seven, as well as an increase in salary from $1,000 to $1,200 annually, which was a good rate by the standards of the time. (When Frances Perkins joined the Consumers League in 1910, she asked for $1,200 but had to settle for $1,000.)[5]

Focus on Italian Women

Most of the victims of the Triangle Shirtwaist Factory were Jewish women from Eastern Europe, but 41 of the 146 were Italian women and teen-age girls. While the disaster had inspired sympathy for those who died, the idea prevailed that immigrants had an adverse impact on the labor market by depressing wages and agreeing to work under conditions not acceptable to Americans. The high number of Italians arriving during the late nineteenth and early twentieth centuries made them a particular target of this resentment. Between 1880 and 1914, more than four million Italians came to the United States. According to the 1910 Census, New York City "had within its boundaries as many persons of Italian stock as Naples, the largest city in Italy." 544,449 of the city's four-and-a-half million residents were born in Italy or were children of Italian-born parents.[6]

Italian women worked primarily in manufacturing—77 percent of those employed—while only 36 percent of all women holding paid jobs in New York City worked in industry; the rest were mostly in domestic service. Previous Russell Sage investigators had heard frequent complaints that "the Italian girl underbids her fellow workers in every occupation she enters ... Italian standards of living are a menace to American industry." The purpose of the new study, according to the introduction, was to "secure exact facts regarding" Italian women in order to determine whether the charges against them were "founded on fact or on a contortion of facts" and what actions "the community might take to remove the causes underlying such charges." Research would also provide insight into "the effect of American industrial and living conditions upon their native standards, and, conversely, the effect of their Italian standards of life and work on the industries they engage in. As such, the study touches the problems both of immigration and of industry."[7] Previous investigations had focused on a particular industry, but the aim of the present one was more ambitious: "The information about [Italian women's] industrial and home conditions should be a contribution to the larger problems of immigration and of women's work."[8]

The Foundation's Committee on Women's Work assigned Louise

and five other investigators to the project, including two who spoke Italian and one medical doctor. Following the methodology used in previous studies, they visited factories, conducted interviews, and recorded the information on pre-printed cards, designed to capture a wide range of information about individual workers, households, budgets, and work places. In her introduction, Louise emphasized that, because several persons were doing field work, "the information gathered has the advantage of representing more than one point of view."[9] She herself pulled it all together and wrote the book, which appeared in 1919, and its conclusions reflect her point of view.

The six researchers established a branch office in the building of the Richmond Hill Settlement, at 28 MacDougal Street, on the opposite side of Washington Square from Waverly Place, the site of the infamous fire. About one third of Manhattan's Italians lived in four neighborhoods below Fourteenth Street, which offered "typical and representative conditions" and "included immigrants from both the north and south of Italy, and recent arrivals as well as families that had been in this country many years."[10] The opening chapter describes the Italian "colonies":

> The name 'Little Italy' is frequently applied to each of these districts. ... They form small communities in themselves, almost independent of the life of the great city. Here the people may follow the customs and ways of their forefathers. They speak their own language, trade in stores kept by countrymen, and put their savings into Italian banks. ... Italian priests minister to their spiritual needs in the Catholic churches, and societies composed only of Italians are organized for mutual aid and benefit. The stores all bear Italian names, the special bargains and souvenirs of the day are advertised in Italian, and they offer for sale the wines and olive oils, 'pasta,' and other favorite foods of the people.[11]

Working Conditions

Most of the women in the study were employed within walking distance of their homes by factories or workshops in the industrial area surrounding the Italian district in Lower Manhattan: "The location of the Italian colony within these industrial boundaries is typical of the bond between its members and the life of the city." Louise and her team investigated 271 of these establishments. Walking along busy streets, lined with high loft buildings and remodeled dwellings, the researchers sniffed "the odor of chocolate from some candy factory or the strong smell of glue from a paper-box plant," heard the noise of heavy-power sewing machines that were shaking "gray buildings of 15 or 20 stories towering high to the heavens," and watched trucks being loaded with "underwear, neckwear, shirtwaists, or mattresses and burial supplies." They ascended narrow, wooden, unenclosed stairs or travelled on slow and rickety elevators (at their own risk, according to the signs posted) to visit crowded workrooms where "clothing is made by the wholesale, hats turned out by the gross, and flowers and feathers pasted, branched, and packed for shipment to the farthest corners of the country."[12] The description of the setting conveys both the author's excitement about the intensity and volume of activity and her critique of the disregard for the wellbeing of the human beings engaged in it.

With few exceptions, the factories had deficient physical conditions. At the recommendation of the Factory Investigating Commission, the New York State legislature had passed laws to prohibit smoking and require fire drills, fire escapes, and sprinkler systems, but only a few employers had introduced the mandatory safety measures. The investigators found "inadequate and dangerous exits; piles of stock in front of windows and doors, the crowding together of machines and chairs so that workers could not pass freely in or out; unprotected gas flames near inflammable material" and emphasized that "it is not enough to have laws upon the statute books providing protection against all these conditions; they must be enforced."[13]

Not only did employers ignore statutes, but they failed to consider inexpensive, common-sense measures such as adequate light and ventilation that might improve both health and productivity. The physician on the investigation team observed that girls in the only "needle trade" factory where ventilation was scientifically controlled "seemed to enjoy their work in spite of its monotony" and looked healthy, without the "stooped shoulders and depressed air of women in other shops where windows could not be opened." Despite the fact that New York law required factories to provide chairs with backs for female workers engaged in tasks that could be performed while sitting, women often stood for ten hours a day, six days a week, steaming feathers, hand-stamping stationery, stripping tobacco, and tending machines. Noise was also an issue. The author commented tersely, "a person can do a higher grade of work when the function of the auditory nerve does not have to be suppressed." Time and again, the investigators emphasized the advantage to employers—as well as employees—of improving working conditions: "The installation of a lunch room or some facilities for providing the workers with a proper lunch is a good paying investment." Not only would stains on fabrics be less likely if workers did not have to eat at their machines, but, after a chance to exercise and get fresh air, employees would return to their stations "with renewed energy and interest."[14]

Why would women put up with such deplorable conditions? The answer was simple—they needed the money:

> For the sake of what her pay envelope contains, [a woman] will sit hour after hour at a sewing machine guiding hundreds of corset covers; at a table piled high with stacks of red and yellow petals to be made into flowers; in an ice-room dipping hundreds of thousands of creams into hot chocolate. She will sort dirty rags until her throat and lungs are choked with dust. She will keep up with the relentless speed of a machine which announces by a ring that 50 paper bags have been pasted and printed and must be removed before the machine can continue. The muscles in her arms are swollen, but there is no pause in the ten-hour day.[15]

The chapter on the pay envelope provides statistics and analysis of wages and their relation to standard of living. The women reported lower weekly rates than those cited by employers, in part because the latter deducted charges for supplies such as needles, spools of thread, even electrical power, and for spoiled goods (a girl who ruined two pairs of gloves lost a week's earnings); they also charged fines for lateness, even when it was due to a malfunctioning elevator or a crowd waiting to punch in at the same time, or when women had worked overtime or at home the night before. The problem of irregularity that Louise had documented in previous studies also reduced annual income. Of the women investigated, 81 percent earned less than $468 a year—the minimum on which a girl eighteen or older could support herself, according to a 1915 estimate, i.e. rent a room and pay for meals, transportation, clothing, and other necessities.[16]

For overtime, mandatory during busy periods, employees usually received only the regular hourly or piece-work pay. The normal work day was long to begin with, often exceeding the maximum recently set by New York State law—54 hours a week. Some women protested that "it is not worthwhile to kill yourself"; they knew the meager additional earnings would not compensate for physical and mental weariness, but economic pressure at home, anticipated "slack times," and the threat of dismissal compelled many to accept. Theresa, a feather maker, "eighteen years old, pale, thin, and anemic, had worked nearly every night until eleven for six weeks. She said she would lose her job if she refused to take the work."[17] Louise referred to Josephine Goldmark's study *Fatigue and Efficiency*, published in 1912, which emphasized that overtime was not only deleterious to workers' health but "economically extravagant" because it reduced productivity and quality of output. A few employers agreed; one said, "You are no good if you work more than nine or so hours a day. Even your head will not work."[18]

In her discussion of vacations and sick leave, Louise emphasized that considering workers' well-being might improve productivity, but, unfortunately, "few employers had realized that a vacation with pay to their workers might benefit the establishment in providing a good rest, new strength and renewed interest in the work." When shops closed for legal holidays like Christmas or New Year's Day, workers lost wages. "Why should I pay for holidays?" one employer objected. Only seventeen percent of the women interviewed took time off for vacations without pay, and most of them reported to work even when they were sick. Women disregarded their physical condition, Louise observed poignantly, because "many had always been accustomed to a low standard of vitality, so that they continued at work when others of different health standards would feel fully justified in remaining at home and taking care of themselves."[19]

The reason why women accepted overtime and did not take leave was the same problem of irregular employment that Louise had observed as a resident at the College Settlement. "In the shops investigated, only about three-fourths of the women employed in the busy season were kept during the slack season." Some firms, she was pleased to notice, recognized the benefit of keeping their workers even during periods when there was little to do and thus avoiding "the expense of hiring and training new help when the busy season came by having a force that understood their methods."[20] Those were the exceptions, however, and most of the women interviewed lived in constant fear of being laid off because their wages were essential for their family's survival.

Home Visits

The Richmond Hill Settlement had developed strong relationships with the residents of the Italian community and facilitated local contacts for the Russell Sage team. Starting in December 1911 and ending in June 1913, Louise and her colleagues made a total of 2,727 calls on 1,095 female wage earners and collected personal details about them and their conditions. They visited the home of each employee at least twice, once during the day to interview her mother about the family and once in the evening to listen to the young woman's own story. Louise seems to have had no worry about her personal safety walking the streets of Lower Manhattan at night. She flirted with the young men that hung around on street corners ("If indeed you could see how the handsome young Italian fellows roll 'dem soulful eyes' at me, you'd think I was still Sweet Sixteen," she told her Barnard classmates), entered halls that were "dark or lighted by a single gas jet," and walked up "rickety wooden stairs, grimy and littered" with the debris and dirt left by hundreds of occupants. The living conditions in the tenements were appalling: "The sole water supply of many, cold at that, was a sink in a public hallway. The majority of families did not have a private toilet, but had to use one in common with others in the tenement ... often filthy, dark and with plumbing out of order. ... Each tenant had to supply his own cook-stove, and some apartments were not even supplied with gas, dangerous oil lamps still being used."[21]

Despite the dismal surroundings, the residents welcomed Louise and enjoyed answering her questions. She had never learned the ethnographic method of participant observation, which involves the investigator studying the life of a group by sharing in its activities, but that is what she was practicing as she joined her subjects for dinner: "It is indeed a life of motleyed experience, drinking wine almost by the quart, eating supper with these people (oh, don't mind if the macaroni is served from a wash bowl in the middle of the table, or that the glass you drink from has not been washed since the last imbiber), trying to persuade Angelina not to take back her good-for-nothing husband when he gets out in 6 months." (Louise did not know that the "wash bowl" was a standard Italian pasta serving dish!) That description, from her 1912 self-report to Barnard, suggests that she went beyond observation to intervention. Indeed she became friends with some of her subjects, especially with those whom she interviewed for several studies. Commenting on these relationships she added, "It is pathetic to find girls remembering you years after you have been to ply them with an hundred questions, and that your friendly visits have been epochs in their lives."[22]

The apartments Louise visited were over-crowded with large families and sometimes lodgers. After dinner, she observed the transformation of the rooms that took place every night: "Every bit of floor space is covered with a great variety of sleeping devices. Folding beds are dragged out from corners, and imposing pieces of furniture that by day appear to be chiffoniers or sideboards become beds for two or three lodgers at night. Even the kitchen, which serves as the common cooking, dining, and living room, and washing place must do service at night as a bedroom. This crowding often means three or four persons to a bed." Congested living quarters increased susceptibility to disease. Tuberculosis was common in the tenements, and the infant mortality rate was high. Most families carried minimal life insurance for all members, including children, so as to be able to afford "the elaborate funeral which is part of the Italian standard of living."[23]

Low wages and irregular employment made it necessary for everyone to contribute to family income. Children, even those of pre-school age, participated in artificial flower-making, as Louise and her colleagues had noted in their study of that trade; older siblings joined the effort after school, and, because they had no time to study, they often fell behind. A 1909 Russell Sage study, entitled "Laggards in Our Schools," showed that 36 percent of Italian school children had to repeat a grade—a higher percentage than any other immigrant group.[24] Family emergencies like the illness or unemployment of a parent caused youngsters to drop out of school and work full-time in violation of the law that set sixteen years as the minimum age for full-time employment. One young woman interviewed had left school at fourteen because "my father wasn't working then. He had stomach trouble. It was hard times at home."[25]

Louise's description of an evening with the Cioffari family captures the impact of child labor: "The family had 'always' made flowers at home, and each small child was taught how to slip [crimp] and paste hideous cotton daisies and violets long before she learned the alphabet." One daughter, ironically named Flora, "had been a problem for both school nurse and visitor." Her sister Philomena had also "been backward in school and ... when she left at the age of fourteen, she was in a special class." When their father explained that both his daughters were "stupid and could not learn anything," Philomena exclaimed, "How could I when I had to work all the time?" The impact on children's physical and mental health extended into adulthood: "Rarely having had the enjoyment and the free movements of play in the fresh air, essential to the healthy development of children, they started on their careers of wage-earning without any real vitality or ambition to succeed ... For the little home worker, all sense of novelty had been worn away from the idea of going to work, and she had had only too full an opportunity of realizing at how little her labor would be valued."[26]

Parents rarely allowed girls to go out at night, thus preventing them from attending evening classes, which might have compensated for their leaving school at fourteen. Neither mothers nor fathers saw the point of girls receiving education: "Why should she go to high school when she's going to be married anyway?" was a typical comment. Women were usually married by the age of twenty-one through an arrangement between parents and not expected to continue working outside the home although economic necessity compelled some to do so. A few girls braved criticism to attend evening school, but prejudice, fatigue, and domestic chores kept most of them away. Typical comments were "too tired evenings to think of going. In evenings have always had to help sister with the housework"; "have to work on flowers at night at home"; "no time after washing dishes and putting down folding beds."[27]

The income of daughters was essential for family survival: "The irregular earnings of the two daughters of the Lombardi family [Mary aged eighteen and Millie seventeen] were the principal source of income for its twelve members, ranging from the father of forty-two, who earned a precarious living by peddling, to the three-week-old baby."[28] Their financial contributions did not, however, enhance girls' status in the family. They were "kept in the paradoxical position of simultaneous wage-earning and dependence" and remained subject to traditional Italian restraints on female conduct.[29] Boys were free to come and go, sometimes with disastrous results: the younger ones might get involved with street gangs, and others became "shiftless ne'er-do-wells" and "drunkards." They usually kept half of their wages for their own purposes while daughters turned over their entire pay envelope to their mothers. "Of course they don't give all they make. They're men and you never know their ways," said one mother. Louise's comment shows less sympathy for those ways: "The Italian girl takes her breadwinning more seriously than does her brother, who, for the most part, is only too ready to throw over his work on slight provocation and loaf around for a while on the plea that he cannot find employment. She feels her responsibility keenly, and slack time is a season of horror to her. 'Last summer when I was laid off for nine weeks, I couldn't sleep nights.' said one girl."[30] Jennie, the Italian flower maker that Louise described to her Barnard classmates, supported three strong, grown brothers, her mother, and herself "because her mother would not leave these sons though they abuse and boss her, and Jennie would not leave her mother."[31]

The home visits allowed Louise to get to know Jennie and the other women she interviewed and to discover how varied were their reasons for emigrating and their experiences in America: "The wife who in revenge was seeking a delinquent husband was found finishing cloaks, while the young woman of twenty-four who had always been 'crazy' to see this country was pressing underwear at $6.00 a week in a factory. ... Two sisters, one eighteen and the other twenty, had come 'to make a dowry.' They were found sorting dusty waste papers and rags in a gloomy basement. Mrs. Cinque, when she was left a widow eleven years before, had immigrated to New York 'to forget her sorrows.'" Despite the hard work and harsh conditions, several of the women found that, they were better off in America than in Italy. There, "Aida, still only a child of fifteen, had had to do all the housework, besides working on the farm: 'I worked like a horse, not like a woman,' she said. She still had her red cheeks and splendid health in spite of the fact that she stood all day as a turner in a dusty bag factory." Another woman had gone to work at the age of twelve in Pavia, where she earned 18 cents in a twelve-hour day. To her, factories in Italy seemed awful. "Here, if you don't like a place, you can always find another."[32]

Louise had begun her study in order to determine the justice of the charges levied against Italian women— that they had a negative impact on the work place and job market and that they were responsible for the dirty and unsanitary conditions under which they lived. She concluded that "the discouraging picture disclosed by following [Italians] into their homes and into their workshops presents an indictment ... not of their personal standards but rather of the social and industrial conditions that are permitted to exist."[33] The living conditions of the women interviewed "seemed to bear a direct relation to their earnings. ... The better paid had better homes, food and clothing. It was only the lower paid who endured the poorer living conditions." Even on a modest income, a single woman interviewed had decorated the room she rented with "gay dishes," bright pictures and a guitar. "The care of her room was a daily joy and her only recreation."[34] Details such as these help the reader see Italian women not as an anonymous group threatening

American values but as individual human beings with hopes and dreams, trying to meet challenges and create new lives for themselves under difficult circumstances.

Challenging the Anti-Immigrant Trend

Although Louise and her team had collected the data by the summer of 1913, they were unable to continue the processing, first, because other Foundation projects took precedence, including co-operation with the Factory Investigating Commission and a major survey requested by the city of Springfield, Illinois, and, later, because Louise herself got a new job. By the time the book appeared in 1919, the political climate had changed. Anti-immigration sentiment and isolationist fears of U.S. involvement in the world had increased since the start of World War I. In response, Congress passed the Immigration Act of 1917, overriding President Wilson's veto. The act excluded individuals from Asia and other categories of "undesirable aliens" (such as "idiots," "anarchists," alcoholics, and prostitutes), imposed a tax on immigrants over the age of sixteen, and required them to demonstrate proof of literacy.

The introduction and conclusion to *Italian Women in Industry* placed the book in this new context. Louise dismissed the literacy requirement of the 1917 act as perfunctory (the immigrant had to "read a few words of his own language … and give a verbal definition of democracy") and stressed the much more important task of integrating new-comers: "We have in our midst thousands of foreigners who must be molded into American citizens and imbued with a sympathetic understanding of our ideals and institutions." Immigration had declined during the war, but she assumed that the return to normal conditions would bring both an increase and "new complexities [as] the hitherto inarticulate peoples of Europe who are now finding voice in public affairs are likely, in any country to which they emigrate, to bring with them for good or ill this new stirring of power." In order to further the "assimilation which is essential if we hope to make our immigration population count in the upbuilding of our nation," we need to help the newcomers "make the readjustments which are necessary in order to fit them into our American life." That process begins with Americans learning about the "foreign born who are now among us ... their work and their play ... their struggles and successes ... their problems and their discouragements."[35] Providing such information was one of the goals of her book.

The final chapter, entitled "Readjustment," took issue even more strongly than the introduction with attitudes and policies prevailing at the time of publication: "We have permitted aliens to live among us for twenty or thirty years who have learned little more about our institutions, our ideals or our standards than they knew when they landed. ... We have not sought to discover what their assets were on their arrival. ... Worst of all, we have let die that ambition and precious spirit of initiative which led these immigrants to come here."[36]

Louise saw herself as a member of the collective "we," but she may also have been thinking about her own parents, who had arrived full of ambition and initiative, learned English, cultivated land in Nebraska and Texas, established themselves as solid middle-class citizens, educated their children, and thus contributed to the "upbuilding of our nation." They had benefitted from the lack of prejudice against Scandinavians, who were thought to be more like Americans than other immigrant groups, and, although they had lived in Swedish communities in Chicago and Nebraska when they first came to the United States, they did not maintain an "ethnic" identity. They were Americans, and their daughter never doubted the superiority of American institutions, ideals, and standards. "We" who were already here needed to share these benefits with the "strong, healthy, and ambitious men and women, who come to this country with a great capacity for work," in order to "weld into a homogeneous nation the foreign with the native population."[37] A twenty-first century reader, used to celebrating diversity, may object to "homogenous" as a desirable outcome while envying Louise and her contemporaries their confidence in the capacity and willingness of American society to absorb and integrate newcomers.

Although Louise acknowledged the growth of negative attitudes towards immigrants, the conclusion of the book strikes an optimistic note. During World War I, the government had established and enforced industrial standards in shops that contracted for war production, including safety, the eight-hour work day, and "wage scales, adequate for a standard of decent living." She hoped that such standards would prevail even more widely in peace time for the benefit of all workers. Shorter hours would make it possible for immigrants to attend evening schools and learn English, and, if they understood government regulations, they would not accept sub-standard conditions of work and thus not underbid native workers. Her conclusion refers to "the troublous period of [postwar] reconstruction" but affirms the basic Progressive commitment to helping the alien *and* the native worker "secure a fair share of the fruits of his labor, under conditions conducive to the enjoyment of them."[38]

The election of 1920 put an end to those hopes and inaugurated a period of increasing restrictions on immigration. *Italian Women in Industry*, however, was well received by professionals in the field. Sophonisba Breckenridge, head of the University of Chicago School of Social Service Administration, appreciated the intent of the book in *Journal of Political Economy*: "Interesting facts with reference to the family discipline indicate a resource in the loyalty and patience of these Italian girls when once a loyalty has been built up and a goal pointed out, from which may be developed a very rich contribution to the life of our American communities."[39] Sociologist Annie Marion MacLean wrote in *American Journal of Sociology* that "Miss Odencrantz has given us a sympathetic and scholarly study."[40] In 1977, the book was re-printed by a publisher who specialized in re-issuing scholarly works on social issues, and it is regularly cited in studies of labor history and immigration.[41]

Chapter VII

Industry Exists for People

Considering the Human Factor in Heavy Industry

The Russell Sage Foundation project that delayed the publication of the study of Italian women was a survey of industrial and social conditions in Springfield, Illinois, requested in 1914 by a group of local citizens. The newly established Department of Surveys and Exhibits coordinated the investigation, joined by staff from the Division of Industrial Studies (which had replaced the Committee on Women's Work) and other sections as well as more than 120 local volunteers. Separate teams focused on each of nine areas. Louise and Zenas Potter, recently hired as "field surveyor," led the investigation of industrial conditions. Potter—two years younger than Louise and the first male colleague with whom she worked—brought to the project his experience as chief inspector of canneries for the New York State Factory Investigating Commission. He was also in charge of examining Springfield's correctional system, so it is likely that Louise was responsible for a major part of the industrial report.

    The introduction to *Industrial Conditions in Springfield, Illinois*, published in 1916, states the basic principles that guided the investigators: "Industry exists for people, not people for industry; and industry can never be considered satisfactory until it serves effectively those who furnish capital and directing ability, those who furnish labor, and those who form the consuming community." This statement contrasts starkly with the focus on maximizing shareholder value that American corporations have embraced as their primary goal since the 1980s.[1]

The authors also make a strong moral argument for a minimum wage: "Workers who give their full working time to an industry should receive as a very minimum a wage which will provide the necessities of life. ... If the business cannot provide this there is serious question whether it has a right to exist." Twenty-first-century discussions about raising the minimum wage tend to focus on the possible impact on employment, but Franklin Roosevelt used language similar to that of the Springfield study when he introduced a proposal in 1933: "It seems to me to be equally plain that no business which depends for existence on paying less than living wages to its workers has any right to continue in this country." (The minimum wage was included in the Fair Labor Standards Act passed in 1938).[2]

Springfield broadened Louise's experience beyond the female workers in light industries that she had investigated in New York. In Illinois, she inspected coalmines, lumber yards, and heavy metal plants, which employed male laborers. With few exceptions, she found the conditions appalling. A photo in the report features a man using a rip saw without a guard to protect his hands from being drawn under the spur wheel and prevent boards from kicking back. Zinc factory fumes caused "zinc chills" and colic, and metal workers, besides enduring the "jarring, shaking and deafening noise" of grinding wheels, were inhaling dust containing sharp particles that caused severe respiratory ailments. Some plants had installed exhaust fans (as required by law), and a photo shows a week's worth of metal dust (nine barrels), which would have been breathed by workers if it had not been removed. Such fans were the exception rather than the rule, and, as a result, "death rates of persons engaged in dusty trades are notably high."[3]

At a time when industrial accidents caused an estimated 40,000 deaths and two million injuries annually in the United States, the numbers recorded in Springfield were not exceptional although the official data probably understated the reality by failing to include causes found on some death certificates (e.g. "struck by falling object" or "injured by fall"). Nevertheless, the investigators found that Illinois was behind many other states with regard to ensuring workplace safety. The few laws enacted did not provide the clarity or resources necessary for effective implementation. They set vague minimal standards such as requiring workshops to have "sufficient and reasonable means of escape," but few shops had fire escapes or fire-fighting equipment, and dust, accumulated boxes and other packing materials often created hazards similar to those that had caused the Triangle fire in New York.[4]

Failure to identify hazards was noticeable in the two industries responsible for the highest number of accidents, coal mining and transportation. Coal mine inspectors provided information about output and equipment but did not mention safety violations. The one railroad safety inspector appointed for the whole state identified defects but was unable to follow up, and he ignored one significant factor: workers' fatigue from excessive hours on duty. Railway engineers and switchmen, exhausted from working ten or twelve hours seven days a week, placed passengers at risk: "Railways are public conveyances and if hours are so long as to cause undue fatigue among the workers, serious mishaps involving not only the workers but the travelling public may result."[5] In order to remedy these and other failures of the system, the report recommended that the state enact statutes that defined functions clearly and provided guidelines and resources for implementation.

Government had an important role in creating and monitoring safety regulations, but the report insisted that "much of the responsibility must go back to" individual employers. By creating safe working conditions, they would not only "gain the respect and goodwill of their employees" but improve their bottom line.[6] Inexpensive measures such as replacing movable wooden ladders by stationary iron ladders and adding railings could prevent many casualties. Good lighting increased production—by as much as ten percent in a Wisconsin steel plant cited in the report. Providing comfortable seating for people whose work did not require standing decreased fatigue and improved morale as well as efficiency. The report commended the Illinois Watch Company for installing chairs on platforms mounted on ball-bearing devices, which allowed women to remain seated while moving between machines, and providing a lunch room, shown in a photo as an example of consideration for worker's welfare. The same company also protected employees during a period of industrial depression by avoiding lay-offs and, instead, reducing daily hours from ten to nine. Managers had expected output to decrease proportionately and were surprised to discover that it only fell by three percent.

Louise's comments on the Illinois Watch Company's practices show her familiarity with the principles of scientific management and the adaptation of these ideas by Progressive reformers. Frederick Taylor (1856-1915), who published *The Principles of Scientific Management* in 1909, had sought ways to eliminate waste in work processes in order to raise profits. His followers, who established the Taylor Society in 1911, recognized that increasing productivity required attention to workers' welfare. The Springfield study references "economic forces only now being discovered and experimented with," which tend "toward increased efficiency and increased production through greater consideration of the human factor in industry. Economies appear to be possible, for example, through shorter working hours that lower the accident rate, and that allow time for recuperation from fatigue; through the elimination of unemployment periods, thus escaping costs due to changes in the labor force; through increased wages ... that would enable workers to raise their standard of living and thus maintain a higher degree of resistance against sickness."[7] Louise and her colleagues had made similar observations in their investigations of women in Manhattan workshops, and Josephine Goldmark had articulated the principles in *Fatigue and Efficiency* (1912). Their ideas entered the mainstream through their integration into the scientific management movement.

The Springfield study applied the methodology that Louise had learned in her previous work for the Russell Sage Foundation: a combination of background research, inspections of work sites, and interviews with individuals in their homes in order to ascertain "the effect of industrial conditions, particularly wages and unemployment, upon family life." For these interviews, she and Zenas Potter selected 100 families, "as nearly representative as possible," a total of 573 persons, of whom 272 were employed, including 27 percent of the mothers, who sometimes left small children unattended while their older siblings were in school. Although Springfield's population was "peculiarly American, 81 percent of its people being American-born whites and another 6 per cent American-born Negroes," living conditions were as deplorable as those of immigrants in New York tenements: Most of the families studied lived in dilapidated four- or five-room frame houses that were in a poor state of repair and had no gas, electricity, city water, or inside toilets. Overcrowding was common; frequently, three generations lived together under the same roof, and some families took in lodgers to help pay the rent.[8]

The home interviews showed that male as well as female laborers in Springfield faced the same issues of excessive working hours, inadequate pay, irregular employment, and unsafe conditions as immigrants in New York with equally destructive effects on health and family life. Descriptions of individuals whose condition had impressed the interviewers illustrate the human consequences. An eighteen-year-old laundry worker complained that, after standing at a mangle for ten hours, "her feet were often so tired and swollen that, in the morning, even after a night's rest, she sometimes cried with pain when attempting to put on her shoes." A boiler-maker often worked thirty-six hours straight, from Saturday morning through to Sunday night, with only time off for meals. "This man had frequently been injured about the face and eyes by bits of flying steel and had had several severe electric shocks." His wife finally asked him to stop working the long hours, even if he did make extra money.[9]

Excessive working hours were related to another problem: irregular employment—the issue that Louise had documented in her master's thesis. Workers had to take long shifts when those were available because they never knew when they would be laid off or because industries were seasonal. Coal mines, for example, closed or operated at reduced capacity during the summer months. Of the families that Louise visited, "only one-fourth reported regular employment for all persons contributing to the family income during the previous year."[10]

Because parents' income was uncertain, 72 percent of children between the ages of fourteen and sixteen worked full-time; their earnings were "absolutely needed for the support of the family."[11] Indeed, many children worked more hours than child labor laws permitted. One fourteen-year-old boy washed bottles, ran errands, and did other odd jobs in a drug store for seven days a week, ten or more hours a day. "He was so tired, his mother stated, that he used to cry after he came home at the end of his day of fourteen hours of work. His mother finally made him quit his job."[12] In New York, Louise had been appalled by preschool children making artificial flowers and doing other kinds of piecework, but at least they stayed in their home. In Springfield, she learned that parents sent boys as young as three to gather bits of coal along the railroad tracks in order to help families reduce fuel costs.

Illinois had child labor laws on the books, but, like the statutes related to workplace safety, they were limited in scope and easy to circumvent. New York mandated completion of sixth grade and a thorough physical exam by a medical officer before allowing children to work, but Illinois had no such requirement. "An anemic or tubercular boy may require fresh air and sunlight, but that fact is no bar to his getting a certificate to work in a Springfield factory or a Chicago sweat-shop. A girl may be sickly and undersized, but that will not prevent her from getting a certificate which will permit her to stand behind a counter from morning till night," the study observed. The minimum age for juvenile employment was fourteen years, but the state accepted an affidavit signed by parents as sufficient proof that their child met the requirement. Children had to be able to "read and write legibly" simple sentences but did not have to demonstrate math skills or even finish elementary school before receiving work certificates.[13] Few of the children found apprenticeships in a trade; most of them worked in menial jobs that provided no training and found themselves trapped in blind-alley occupations.

While many parents saw no option but to take their children out of school, some made great sacrifices for their children. Mindful, perhaps, of the benefits she had derived from her own parents' commitment to education, Louise acknowledged a "colored family" in which "two girls, fifteen and sixteen years of age ... continued in school although the father was a day laborer and the mother had to work out by the day to supplement his earnings. The mother was anxious that her children should be educated."[14] (That, incidentally, is one of the few references to African-Americans in the published study; it is surprising that the survey does not mention race relations in view of the 1908 Springfield riot, an incident of mass racial violence, which inspired the creation of the National

Association for the Advancement of Colored People the following year.)

Historian and social critic Christopher Lasch has criticized the "planners and policy-makers" of the Progressive movement for their "invasion of family life" and their insistence that "the family could not provide for its own needs without expert intervention."[15] His argument misses the point that what reformers wanted to change were the economic and social conditions that prevented families from providing for their own needs and being active members of their community. Children who dropped out of school to work at menial jobs did not get the skills and knowledge they needed as future citizens. For the state to cut short their education was "not only short-sighted but thoroughly deplorable," and the easy circumvention of statutes regarding child labor encouraged children "at an impressionable age to look upon the law as a thing a clever person can evade with impunity."[16] As adults, they would continue to work excessive hours and thus not have time to maintain the interest in public affairs that a healthy democracy requires.

Community Support

The citizens of Springfield, who had commissioned the investigation, shared its basic assumptions. They knew their city had problems and accepted the principle that "the public has a stake in industrial questions and should shoulder its responsibility."[17] The published version of the study defined what that responsibility entailed: support for laws that regulated working hours, child labor, workplace safety, and minimum wages *and* for the enforcement of such legislation. The authors believed that public opinion would "make it hard for industries and commercial enterprises maintaining conditions below a reasonable standard to do business in the community." They looked forward to the creation of "bureaus of government research, committees and commissions on public efficiency," which together with "consumers' leagues, civic improvement societies, and an independent press" would keep citizens informed and thus enable citizens to take control of their lives. Twenty-first-century populists are skeptical of experts and other "elites" including journalists, but Louise and her contemporaries had faith in the cooperation between civic associations and public agencies and believed that "the community [would] be willing and expect to bear its share of the legitimate cost of maintaining good industrial standards."[18]

The response to the survey seemed to justify the authors' optimism. In November, immediately after the completion of the field work, 600 local citizens helped present the results, tabulated and analyzed by Russell Sage staff, at a grand exhibition in the Illinois State Armory, which more than 15,000 visitors attended. The purpose of the event was "to present the major findings of the survey in such simple, graphic, and entertaining ways as to gain the attention of and be understood by the great body of people of the city ... [and to create] a center where, as in a church or a civic society, people could consider an important subject *together*."[19]

The poet and Springfield native Vachel Lindsay reviewed the event enthusiastically in *The Survey*. Reading his article makes a twenty-first-century reader nostalgic for a time when a diverse group of Americans could come together, confident that they could solve problems if they understood them and cooperated. Lindsay's list of participants in the exhibition is comprehensive: "Politicians of the old school and the new, society ladies, religious ladies, miners, Socialists, near-Socialists, stand-patters, lawyers, physicians, preachers ... Most every thinking, arguing person in Springfield has seen, thought, and argued about the show. It has been a pleasant open forum. Each type of opinion has had its chance in the booths or in front of them," and "every main phase of the city's life was here represented."[20]

The exhibit featured "many mechanical devices elaborated by the city's best amateur artists and mechanics. There was a row of charmingly wrought little card-board street-buildings—the dance hall, the saloon, the 'furnished rooms building,' the vaudeville house, and the movie emporium all lit up while the cardboard church and school-buildings were dark." The exhibit organizers were committed to improving local morals and confident that improvement was possible. In a display, drawn from Zenas Potter's report on the correctional system, a "photograph of the jail bull pen lifted up and showed a picture of a farm where the man arrested was working out his penance and perhaps his salvation, under humane conditions."[21]

Each of the areas investigated (charities, the correctional system, schools, industrial conditions, etc.) had its own exhibit booth featuring a loud and enthusiastic "explainer," as well as "cardboard panels lettered in a style plainly read, and cleverly illustrated." Louise's published report reproduced one such panel on women's wages. It quoted a manager who hired "girls who live at home because a girl can't pay board on what she gets and not go wrong or steal" and insisted that the weekly wage of $3.50-$5 was fair because "clerking in a 5&10 cent store is an apprenticeship." "But what do they learn?" the panel asked in capital letters: "They don't make out sales checks. They don't judge or select goods. They don't display articles for sale."[22] The investigators also used drama to show the impact of the conditions they had observed. The most popular feature of the exhibition was a stage on which school children acted in mini-plays dealing with social problems; a photo of a scene from one of them accompanies Lindsay's article. Drawn from the study of industrial conditions, the play features a workingman who had lost his job. "His wife found work, but the home had suffered and the boy ran wild."[23] Louise, who loved the theater, must have been pleased that her report had provided the plot.

Lindsay predicted that the event would have a lasting impact: "Five or six years hence people will be working on public policies that began in the recommendations of the various booths in the state armory."[24] Springfield did in fact enact some of the improvements recommended by the survey, especially in education, charity involvement, and law enforcement, and the plan published by the Illinois Efficiency and Economy Commission in 1915 included the consolidation of the numerous independent bodies dealing with labor conditions that the study recommended. The mood and priorities of the country, however, were changing as World War I continued, eventually involving the United States, and the Foundation turned its attention to urgent special inquiries connected with the war while many staff members left to assume war-related assignments. Louise's career also took a new turn.

Chapter VIII

Connecting Women with Jobs

Entering Public Service

"I never will forget that day. We were in a dirty old building with no heat and were confronted with long lines of people looking for jobs. Two hundred people, with one job to offer, and that housework!" Twenty years later, that was how Louise recalled January 2, 1915, the day the New York City Bureau of Employment opened in an abandoned bank office at 262 Fulton Street in Brooklyn. The interview with the *Barnard College Alumnae Monthly*, quoted here, cites "the entertaining story of how Miss Odencrantz came originally to be connected with the New York State Employment Service" which she "told with the keen sense for the comic that is one of [her] most delightful characteristics. At first the examination for this branch of the civil service was open only to men, but after some agitation it was opened to women. This accomplished, the people responsible were faced with the grim possibility that no women would apply, so Miss Odencrantz was asked as a special favor to take the examination."[1]

Actually, Louise had been working on employment issues for some time. An economic downturn, beginning in early 1914 and aggravated by the outbreak of war the following summer, caused a rise in unemployment. Responding to the situation, the Russell Sage Foundation sponsored discussions among private philanthropic employment agencies, chaired by Mary Van Kleeck, with Louise as secretary. In October 1914, the group asked the latter to draw up a plan for the possible establishment of a clearing house to which agencies might refer calls from employers with unfilled jobs.

Meanwhile, the New York State legislature had responded to the crisis by creating a State Bureau of Employment and instructing the Commissioner of Labor to recruit heads of branch offices through a civil service exam.

When the state offered her a position as superintendent of the New York City Employment Bureau's women's section, Louise faced a major decision. Until that point, her career had followed a straight line from the fellowship at the College Settlement through a series of increasingly responsible positions at the Russell Sage Foundation. Accepting a public sector job would push her in a different direction, and the choice was not straightforward. New York public administration had a reputation for corruption and cronyism, and, as she told the interviewer for the Barnard journal, "everybody consulted in connection with this momentous step was very discouraging, the consensus of opinion being that one only lowered her standards by going into state work."[2]

Louise did, however, know and respect the newly appointed director of the state agency, Charles Barnes, formerly a special investigator for the Russell Sage Foundation and a member of the New York State Factory Investigating Commission. Pauline Goldmark, whom Louise knew through the network of women connected with the Russell Sage Foundation and the National Consumers League and who had served on the Commission with Barnes, advised her to take the job, saying that "if people continued to refuse to go into state work for fear of lowering their standards, the standards would never be raised." The challenge implicit in the recommendation helped persuade Louise, according to the interviewer: "the familiar pioneer urge, thus buttressed, won out," and she accepted the offer.[3] After seven years of investigating conditions and calling attention to problems in the hope that others would solve them, she would have an opportunity to *do* something to change people's lives.

New York State had authorized the employment bureau but allocated few resources. The abandoned bank building in Brooklyn lacked not only heat but basic office furniture such as file cabinets. "We did our filing by the 'shoebox system,' having discovered that a man's shoe box was just the right size for our cards; we haunted the shoe stores of the neighborhood collecting them," Louise told her interviewer.⁴ The 5x8 cards, similar to those that she had used in investigations for the Russell Sage Foundation, recorded personal data, experience, skills, and the position sought. Later, she introduced a system of color coding to help match applicants with vacancies.

The shoe-box approach might be primitive, but it was an important first step towards establishing the structures that existing state employment agencies lacked. In Springfield Louise had observed such an office where "those in charge ... had no real information as to the number of positions actually secured for workers" because they recorded only applications that resulted in referrals and treated referrals as "positions secured" regardless of whether they resulted in actual hires. There was no system of record-keeping: "As soon as application blanks had been entered in the register prescribed by law, the blanks were piled—not filed—in a store room where they had been accumulating since the office was opened five years before."⁵

Besides creating procedures, the employment office faced the challenge of gaining the trust of employers and skilled applicants. According to social historian Ray Lubove, "Employers refused to patronize [such agencies] on the grounds of their inability to provide superior workers, while skilled workers remained aloof because they did not wish to be classified with the general run of applicants attracted to the public office." The depressing atmosphere of the bureaus, which were "dirty and unattractive" and "generally located on dingy streets," was a further disincentive.⁶

Charles Barnes recognized the challenge implicit in the perception of public employment offices "merely as places to handle common labor, or else to cater to the unemployable or near-unemployable" and emphasized the importance of "personality in selecting superintendents and other helpers. Dealing with all sorts of people requires a sympathy and understanding and a tact which is not possessed by many otherwise able persons."⁷ His appointment of Louise as head of the Brooklyn office women's section suggests that he saw she had those qualities, developed through her years of interviewing workers and employers for the Russell Sage Foundation.

Louise was well aware of the need to overcome the prejudice against public employment offices and used every opportunity offered by press coverage to educate readers. The new bureau received a fair amount of publicity. Brooklyn was proud to have been chosen as the location: "Borough to be center from which Movement will be extended" *The New York Herald* announced in its Brooklyn section on January 10, 1915. (The article is accompanied by several photos including one of Louise, sitting at her roll-top desk, a shoebox of cards in front of her, turning towards the reader with an expression of concern that must have re-assured her clients. Not surprisingly, she looks tired—the first week at the agency must have been exhausting.)[8]

The New York City office was the only one in the state that had a separate section serving female applicants, and the uniqueness of a civil service unit consisting "entirely of women and of experts" made a good story. The fact that the superintendent, whose photo accompanied most of the articles, was an attractive young woman from a respected ethnic background, added to the appeal: "Miss Louise Odencrantz, comes of transplanted Scandinavian stock and is justly proud of a pioneering aunt, who was one of the first women to take the degree of doctor of philosophy at a Swedish university."[9]

Louise's statements to the public emphasized that the bureau was not a charitable institution but purely a business proposition: "People seem to think that all the misfits and inefficient people of the city can come to us and find employment. Of course we can't find positions for them, and employers who have the same idea will not apply for help because they think they will not get first-class workers."[10] The term "misfit" sounds harsh, but she used the word in its archaic, literal meaning, "something that does not fit or that fits badly," not in a derogatory sense. She listened with sympathy to everybody who came to her and referred those she could not serve to charitable agencies where they might find help, but her main focus was on identifying applicants' skills and guiding them towards appropriate areas, including some they might not have thought of: girls looking for jobs in offices or department stores might find that, in some cases, factory work offered better wages and working conditions.

Educating employers was equally important. Many of these came to the bureau in search of domestic help, but applicants found the terms offered by industry (such as defined hours of service, specific tasks, and independent living) more appealing. Emulating those conditions would make domestic work more attractive: "If there was more of a business relation between mistress and maid, I firmly believe that the work would be done better and that a class of women would take it up," Louise told the *Brooklyn Eagle*. She cited the example of a former sales clerk in a department store who was hired for general housework and far exceeded her employer's expectations because she applied the business methods she had learned in her former job.[11] Domestic service accounted for about forty per cent of placements, but the 2,055 positions that the bureau had filled by December 1915 included "stenographers, bookkeepers, clerical workers, factory hands, garment workers, dressmakers, saleswomen, teachers, even motion picture theater singers" as well as "positions for college women, hotel and institution managers, store managers, private secretaries, and linguists with half a dozen languages at their tongues' tips."[12]

The ability to serve a large, diverse group of clients was remarkable in view of the dismal space occupied by the bureau, "a big bare room half full of women ... old and young, stupid and intelligent, fat and thin, shabby and prosperous" according to the *New York Tribune*, which commented on Louise's ability to convey both authority and genuine interest in job seekers: "In the center of all this movement Miss Odencrantz sat at her orderly desk, asking questions, answering questions and playing a complicated catalogue game with blue and red and yellow cards—a game that always seemed to solve itself at the first deal. ... Whenever [she] or her assistant dealt with any matter they invariably spoke with the directness and courtesy which come only from a full understanding of the situation." Through her competence and personality, she was able to transform the barren space into "a marketplace to which a woman brings her capacity to work and where the employer comes to contract for work."[13] Another reporter commented on the combination of a carefully planned system of records with personal attention and "constant experience in sizing up and selecting applicants." The use of special tests to determine the ability of clerical workers enabled the Bureau to place workers appropriately, or, as Louise herself summarized her achievement: "minimize the number of misfits in industry."[14]

In March 1916, *The New York Times Magazine* published an article by Louise with the title: "State's First Employment Bureau a Success." Quoting figures for both male and female sections of the bureau, she reported that, since its opening in January 1915, the office had registered almost 24,000 applicants, and employers had sent in calls for more than 10,000 workers. In the course of the first fourteen months, nearly 6,000 people had found jobs, and the rest of the positions, she emphasized, were still in process. That final point was important: Unlike other agencies, which "merely sift from among the applicants the needed help for the job, while those not needed are thrown aside ... the ideal Public Employment Bureau [continues its efforts] until the applicant is finally placed." Her goal was to "diminish the waste and inefficiency of the present methods" of filling jobs.[15] (Although she did not mention this in the article, analysis of the figures cited there and elsewhere indicates that the placement rate for women was about 46 percent while that for men was around 18 percent. The fact that there were fewer female than male job-seekers might facilitate efficiency; also, there were more domestic openings available for women.)

The experience in recording and organizing information that Louise had developed in her previous work served her well in the very different task of supervising an employment bureau and matching applicants with jobs, but, trained as a social scientist, she looked beyond those immediate practical objectives. The data she collected were indicative of trends and might serve as a basis for future developments: "A public employment bureau, if it is to live up to its name and be of public service, must not only serve as a clearing house ... It must also be a bureau of information about the labor market and industrial conditions. In the records that the Brooklyn office is accumulating is a great store for people who are trying to work out problems of industrial betterment."[16] Practice informed theory, and theory supported practice.

Busy as she was, Louise did not have much time for introspection, but an article she wrote for the *Evening Journal* provided a rare opportunity. Published on January 22, 1916, under the heading

"How I Discovered Myself" with the subtitle "Another Successful Woman Tells of Her Work," the article describes her progress in self-deprecating terms: "I have really been so interested in other women that I haven't had time to think about myself. So many of us don't think at all of the fact that we are doing things in the world. We just go ahead and do what seems to be required and never stop to think what would happen or who else would be in our places if things hadn't just happened the way they did."[17]

Feminist scholars have pointed out that "well into the twentieth century, it continued to be impossible for women to admit into their autobiographical narratives the claim of achievement, the admission of ambition. ...[They] report encounters with what would be the life's work as having occurred by chance." Louise's statement shows the same modesty ("if things hadn't just happened the way they did"), but it says something else about the way women of her generation developed their careers. They did not start their professional lives by defining a specific personal goal but by observing the world, seeing its needs, and doing "what seems to be required." Following that process, Louise had discovered what she was called to do: "I trained for a teacher of Latin, but surely nothing could be more different than the work I am doing now. Of course I believe that it was meant to be that way. Even though I began my work in the employment bureau without much of an idea of what I was about to undertake, I know now that it meant the foundation of my life work."[18] It is remarkable for a thirty-one-year-old woman to think in terms of a "life-work" — especially at a time when few women pursued professional careers. She was, however, fulfilling the expectations of Emily Putnam, the first head of Barnard, who had said, "We are interested in opening every sort of opportunity to women, and then we shall quickly discover what women can do."[19]

In the *Evening Journal* article, Louise credits her success to her sense of humor (a quality she had inherited from her Danish mother, whose memoirs captured the amusing side of her hard and dangerous life as a Nebraska pioneer): "One thing above all others has carried me through many a dark and gloomy place, and that is my sense of humor. Here at my desk I listen, day in and day out, to the troubles and cares of other women. I wish that more women would try to see the humor in their different troubles." Her sense of humor made it possible to get through difficult days ("if I have a particularly trying day, I forget it when I go home and think of frivolous things to make me laugh"), but, more importantly, it enabled her to perceive incongruities and thus discover hidden possibilities: "I have really applied humor to cases that looked blackest and found some responsive glimmer of hope somewhere hidden that might not have come to light at all otherwise. Humor spells renewed vigor." (The quality of "vigor" to her encompassed not only physical and intellectual energy but vision and imagination. She had criticized the employment bureau in Springfield for its "lack of vigor and grasp of possibilities.")[20]

Louise was especially committed to helping very young girls who had left school at fourteen and obtained working papers but were not qualified for any job. "Lots of young people came into the office, and we began to develop the techniques of vocational guidance and testing, all very new," she told the Barnard interviewer later.[21] Recognizing that training these applicants and helping them find work required greater resources than her office could provide, she advocated for a public agency dedicated to their needs and served as chair of the Committee on Vocational Guidance of the Woman's Municipal Service. An April 4, 1916, headline in the *Evening Post*— "Urges a Children's Bureau: Miss Odencrantz Wants State to Create Separate Employment Agency" —suggests that she was gaining recognition as an authority on employment policies in New York. The following year, she assembled a committee that presented a bill to the legislature providing for the first Junior Division of the New York State Employment Service.[22]

Besides promoting job counseling, Louise advocated an end to the evil of child labor, including the homework system that she had observed during her investigations of the artificial flower industry and of Italian households. "Deprived of the opportunity for normal play and physical development in the open air, confined in the house and working in poorly ventilated rooms, often under pressure of speed, discouraged by poor progress in school through no fault of their own, the children do not have a fair start when they enter their wage-earning years," she wrote in 1917, pointing out the irony that "when the declaration of war brought a sudden demand for national emblem pins, children were found in the tenements engaged in fastening the pins on the emblem of democracy and freedom."[23]

At the time, it looked as if opponents of child labor were gaining ground. In September 1916, Congress had passed the Keating-Owen Act, prohibiting interstate trading of products from factories that employed children under the age of fourteen and mines that employed those under sixteen, but the Supreme Court declared the law unconstitutional in 1918. It would be another twenty years before Congress regulated the labor of sixteen-to-eighteen-year-olds as part of the 1938 Fair Labor Standards Act.

Meeting War-Time Needs

The entry of United States into World War I in April 1917 had an immediate impact on the activities of the employment bureau. As war production increased and men joined the military, the demand for female labor grew significantly. A year earlier, Louise had mentioned women chauffeurs and elevator runners as a novelty or a joke; now women were becoming a familiar sight not only in such positions but in industrial plants throughout the country. According to historian Alice Kessler-Harris, "World War I allowed women to demonstrate aptitude for certain 'inappropriate' jobs. ... In entering new fields, women challenged the physiological and social assumptions that justified discrimination against them. Employers registered surprise at women's ability to do jobs previously denied them."[24]

In June 1917, a move to better facilities than the old bank enabled the employment bureau to respond more effectively to the increasing demands. The new office was in an attractive brick-and-stone building, centrally located, near Borough Hall, the administrative center of Brooklyn, and a few minutes' walk from all the principal subway, surface, and elevated car lines. The women's department was on the second floor and had a separate entrance and space where staff could talk confidentially with applicants, unlike the old location where all conversations took place in the large open office. In her report to the New York State Industrial Commission, Louise described the new setting enthusiastically: "The lighting, heating and ventilating facilities are excellent, and the rooms are kept clean and attractive. We know of no public employment office in the United States with better facilities for its applicants or more attractive arrangements for its office staff."[25]

The new location enabled the women's department to meet the increased demand for labor, but matching demand and supply was a challenge. Industry required trained workers, but many of the applicants who came to the office lacked the relevant skills. As husbands joined the army, mature women who had worked at home as housewives and mothers suddenly had to earn a living, but many had no previous job experience. Louise put a positive spin on the challenge in an interview with the *Brooklyn Daily Eagle,* which appeared under the headline "Chance for Middle-Aged Women in Ranks of City Wage Earners."[26] By offering training and advising she could prepare these "semi-dependent" women for the labor market.

Another group faced obstacles over which she had no control. She told the state legislature that "the problem of the colored woman worker is serious in New York City. Practically all lines are closed to them except domestic work. At times employers will admit them but usually at lower wages, and at work for which it is difficult to get white help. Moreover, as soon as white help is available, the colored is laid off. The problem of extending the field of employment for colored girls needs serious consideration." There is no record of a response to her urgent appeal, but it is clear that she knew about ongoing efforts to address the issue. Promoting "employment according to ability" for "colored citizens" was one of the goals of the NAACP, founded by Progressive leaders including Jane Addams and Florence Kelley.[27]

Among the war-related assignments that Louise embraced with particular enthusiasm was recruiting urban women to work on farms. Agriculture had been losing laborers to industry for some time, and the Army's demand for manpower raised the shortage to critical levels. The United States needed not only to sustain but to increase food production in order to feed its own population and supply its allies. In May 1917, the New York City Mayor's Committee of Women formed a standing committee on agriculture, chaired by the Dean of Barnard College, Virginia Gildersleeve. Louise joined the group along with eight other members, one of whom cited her contribution: "The cooperation of the women's division of the State Employment Bureau was secured under the able direction of Miss Louise Odencrantz."[28]

The committee recruited seasonal laborers for New York farms and set up residential camps throughout the state, where a diverse group of college students and alumnae, workers laid off during slack season, and others stayed while working nearby. At first, farmers were reluctant to employ female laborers, but the women's ability to carry out all the regular activities of farmhands—ploughing, planting, weeding, harvesting fruit and grain, feeding pigs and milking cows—overcame the initial skepticism, and, by mid-July, their demand for workers exceeded the supply.

Organizers of the effort had expected that those with a college education would become team leaders while factory workers would show greater physical strength. According to the *Barnard Bulletin*, however, "the college girls were found to be the most husky young animals fit for the hardest labor, and the trade school girls displayed splendid executive power." The urban factory workers benefited from a summer of good nutrition, fresh air and exercise, and Louise was pleased to report that they "felt more physically fit and in better health after the season's work, and the great majority were anxious to return a second season."[29]

In the fall of 1917, the so-called "farmerettes" inspired the creation of a voluntary association, the Women's Land Army (WLA), to fill the demands of the next growing season. The governor of New York, Charles Whitman, instructed the employment bureau to work with the WLA. The fact that the latter was a voluntary association while the bureau was a public agency created a certain tension. According to historian Elaine Weiss, "Gildersleeve mediated between Ida Ogilvie [Barnard professor, and leader of one of the camps] representing the WLA, and Louise Odencrantz ... to 'adjust relations' and coordinate the two bodies' work." It is unlikely that Louise, an active and loyal alumna of Barnard, had difficulty cooperating with representatives of her alma mater, but apparently the middle-class members of the WLA had concerns about the "farmerettes" enrolled by the employment bureau: Were they "motivated more by a paycheck than by patriotism? Did they undertake land service as a duty or just another job? Did they bring the same enthusiasm for the work and spirit to the camp?"[30]

The farmers did not share these concerns, and even those who had initially doubted women's ability to do agricultural labor abandoned their skepticism. Between May and October 1918, they submitted requests for 7,738 women workers, and the employment bureau placed more than 3,000. Returning from an inspection visit to up-state New York in June 1918, Louise was happy to report that "the very farmers who were most bitterly opposed to the idea in March are heart and soul for it now," and that, contrary to expectations, women had adjusted to the physical demands of the work, and "deserters" were few and far between.[31] She collected photos of cheerful "farmerettes," dressed in overalls and boots, working in the fields and handling agricultural implements expertly. On the back of some of the pictures—included among her materials at the Schlesinger Library—she herself has written the date and location, suggesting her personal engagement in this project. She was pleased to enable "factory girls" to serve the war effort and happy that women "coming from the crowded parts of a city" gained "health and strength and would return better fitted for their regular work."[32]

During 1918, Louise also served on the Executive Committee of the Clearing House for War Time Training for Women, which published two guides to training opportunities in New York City, one in June and another one in December. The second "bulletin" included a catalog of courses in a wide range of academic and practical subjects—from "aeroplane mechanics" and the Armenian language to bacteriology, statistics, and "wireless telegraphy." The authors did not mention the ongoing debate in Congress about passage of the Nineteenth Amendment, but they provided implicit support for the suffragists' efforts: "One of the increasingly valuable and undeveloped assets of our country at the present moment is its woman power. Translated into an army of skilled and contented workers this power could help enormously in the task of strengthening the second line of defense."[33]

The members of the Clearing House Committee were certain that the demand for women in many fields would continue or even increase after the war. "Nurses are needed not only for service overseas but to fill the depleted ranks in this country, in civil and army hospitals, in public health work, in factories, and in administrative and teaching positions," and because of the high death rate among physicians, women "will be needed to fill the ranks in this field of service." Pharmacy was another area with many openings, and "there never was a time when scientific women had the unrestricted opportunity to prove their ability which is offered them today." The Department of Agriculture needed chemists and biochemists, the Bureau of Standards and public utilities corporations needed physicists, and demand for geologists, entomologists, and plant pathologists was increasing as were requests for laboratory assistants in many fields. To meet these needs, "certain institutions which have heretofore excluded women are opening their courses to them," and the Committee was confident that the principles of "equal training opportunities for women and a single wage scale" would prevail.[34]

Trade schools needed to provide "to the younger girls, the industrial workers of the future, a more fundamental and thorough preparation for industry than is now available."[35] The catalogue also recommended the creation of so-called "vestibule schools," dedicated rooms or shops, where instructors taught procedures and helped workers adjust to factory conditions under less stressful conditions than inside the plant. Louise had seen the benefit of on-site training in her work at the employment bureau and continued to recommend it, e.g. in a speech to an educational congress at the State University of New York at Albany in 1919: "Such gradual introduction would do much to help retain workers after they are hired."[36]

While she was engaged in these civic activities, Louise also took on additional responsibilities in connection with her day-time job. In June 1918, at President Wilson's request, the U.S. Employment Service (USES), the central industrial agency for the country, joined forces with the Bureau of Employment of the New York State Industrial Commission, and Louise became assistant to the Federal Director on Women's Work and supervisor of the women's division of the State of New York employment services. In November, she told an interviewer, "Our personnel, which started with 100, now numbers 500, and our officers have increased from nine to fifty-four, twenty-six in New York City and twenty-eight up State."[37]

That interview was one of four that she gave during the month of November. Evidently, she had become a go-to source for comments on the current employment situation. On November 2, 1918, she told the *New York Tribune* that, just during the previous week, she could have placed about 10,000 women in a broad variety of jobs: "There is work for all, almost without age-limit. Little physical strength and skill is required in many of the assembling processes in the munitions plants, while for some other functions college trained, active women are needed." She was certain that "the draft will take many more men. They must be replaced, or the industries are bound to suffer. It is the women of leisure and the women with little home responsibility who must answer this call to make certain victory possible."[38]

The Armistice concluded on November 11 created a new situation, but Louise was certain that the development of peacetime industries would compensate for the cessation of war-related production. In a November 14 interview with The *Evening Sun* for an article on "Woman's Future in Industry," she expressed her confidence that destitute Europe would need supplies, and pent-up demand for consumer goods would revive the domestic market: "People who for the last two years have been 'making things do' can now buy furniture and china with a clear conscience. ... Our great problem is to redirect labor into what we have been calling non-essential industries without wasting time of employers or employees or causing disappointment and hardship to men and women suddenly thrown out of work." Louise assumed that women would return to traditional jobs such as teaching once the "right proportion of teachers' pay to the pay of industrial workers" was established, implying that, having earned more working in a factory than teaching in a school, women were less likely to accept salaries at the pre-war level. The ability to earn more money, demand an eight-hour day, "or even the much talked-of right to vote" were, however, less important outcomes of women's wartime experience than "the chance to hold down a job demanding responsibility. Hitherto women have received jobs that didn't count. But during the war they learned that a job can be more than a means of earning money, and that the skill and interest displayed count as much as pay."[39] The belief that the purpose of working was not just to earn a living but to find personal fulfillment motivated Louise throughout her career.

The expectation that women would hold the ground they had gained in industry was not fulfilled. A study of post-war conditions concludes that "the emergency expansion of industrial production, and the momentary absence of men, did not alter patterns of employment in manufacturing beyond the war years. With few exceptions, jobs returned to male control when the conflict ended."[40] Women did, however, advance in some areas. The demand for consumer goods created additional jobs—with improved conditions—in retail sales and related fields, and the post-war economy increased the need for telephone and telegraph operators, clerks, and bookkeepers—jobs previously held by women, many of whom had left civilian work for government service.

Employers, Louise predicted, would be delighted to welcome skilled office workers to replace the less competent ones that had filled positions during the war, and the task of the employment office would be to guide those made redundant into suitable positions: "It will be one of my jobs to do away with this office snobbery. I am going to show them that it is better to be a good factory worker than a 'bum' stenographer."[41] She was aware, however, that many women would lose industrial jobs when the men returned to civilian life and believed that public-private cooperation was necessary to assist these women in finding alternative positions. In a January 1919 interview, she cited the example of an ammunition factory on Long Island, which notified the Employment Service that 400 women would be laid off. The Service opened a branch office in the plant, registered the women, and "so far as possible placed them before they had left their positions."[42]

Others shared Louise's hope that cooperation between industry and government agencies would continue. In the spring of 1919, the Russell Sage Foundation initiated studies to capture the wartime experience of operating national systems of public employment offices. Director John Glenn invited "outstanding students of unemployment and pioneer administrators of public employment bureaus"[43] to assist, including Louise, her boss, Charles Barnes, and W.M. Leiserson, who was gaining a reputation as industrial negotiator and labor relations scholar and would play a role in drafting

New Deal legislation, including the Social Security Act of 1934. At the age of thirty-four, with just four years of experience in the field, Louise joined a distinguished group of specialists! They all shared the confidence, which she expressed in a March 1919 interview with the *Evening Post*, that a new era had arrived—not because of government regulations but because of an awakening of public conscience:

> There is a slowly growing understanding that the day of shifting responsibilities on other shoulders is past. We are facing an awakening to civic power, for which the woman's vote has undoubtedly added great impetus. ... The individual man and woman must be brought in direct contact with the Government, with the business of the nation. ... I favor any widespread movement for the education and formation of a public conscience. The sooner we start the sooner we will come to the moment when an awakened people will demand and get the use of orderly methods in an orderly way.[44]

As concrete evidence of this process, Louise cited the emergence of community councils, in which people gathered to discuss their local problem and look for solutions in cooperation with private and public organizations. Such councils were not "a philanthropic undertaking foisted on an unwilling and uninterested neighborhood; it is the organization of local forces coming from within itself." Her statement reflects the Progressives' faith in people's ability to solve their own problems through civic engagement.

The expectation that the passage of the Nineteenth Amendment in 1919 would lead to a general awakening of public conscience and commitment was disappointed as were other hopes of the Progressive Era. Funding for the systems that Louise and her colleagues had created declined before the end of the year. The federal government slashed appropriations, and New York State closed several offices in order to pay for the ones that stayed open. Additional budget cuts would follow in 1921-22, making it almost impossible for the employment service to continue. The cutbacks were part of a general trend. Historian Michael McGerr argues that "World

War I marked the high point of the progressive movement ... [but] was also its death knell." Tired of the "burdens and sacrifices that the wartime government imposed on them," frustrated by the doubling of the cost of living between 1914 and 1920, and frightened by a surge in labor militancy after the Armistice, Americans abandoned the communitarianism of the reformers and their efforts to rein in big business and elected Warren Harding.[45]

The spirit of Progressivism, however, did not disappear but continued to inspire concerned individuals, who found new outlets for their efforts.[46] Accepting responsibility for "the business of the nation" and insisting on using "orderly methods in an orderly way," these citizens—many of them women—would continue to transform local government, voluntary organizations, and even private industry, where Louise found her next job.

Chapter IX

Finding New Outlets for the Progressive Spirit

Applying Common Sense to the Silk Industry

The description of Louise's new job in her work resumé looks formidable: "Personnel manager in charge of employing, training, promotions, wage adjustments, services and industrial relations in three factories in New York, Paterson, N.J., and Pennsylvania with a total of 750 employees when busy."[1] Her career changed direction—as it had in 1915 when she took a government job—but once again, she drew on previous experience and found continuity. The ideas that led Smith & Kaufman Inc., silk manufacturers, to create the position of personnel manager were those she had mentioned in her study of industrial conditions in Springfield: attention to "the human factor" would increase efficiency and output. Mary Van Kleeck, head of the Russell Sage Foundation Division of Industrial Studies and an early member of the Taylor Society, was convinced that the problem of unemployment could be solved by combining the empirical examination of the work process, advocated by scientific management, and attention to the role of individual human beings in that process, which was the purview of social work. She encouraged the fusion of the two fields in the new profession of personnel management and advocated the appointment of women in that role.[2] It is likely that she encouraged Louise to apply for the position with Smith & Kaufmann.

Louise stayed in touch with her mentor and sent her copies of the agreements and other documents she worked on, seeking feedback and advice. Van Kleeck kept the papers and included them with the records she deposited in the Smith College Archives. The two appeared together at a conference of the International Association of Public Employment Services in Ottawa in September 1920. Their topics reflect the difference between their perspectives: Van Kleeck discussed theory ("Research as a Factor in Industrial Relations" was the title of her speech) while Louise spoke in practical terms about the value of cooperation between public employment services and personnel managers: "What we do need now are concrete definite suggestions as to how the two can actually work together." She was convinced that "the ultimate success of any system will depend upon the methods of co-operation that the service can work out on the one side with employers and on the other with workers."[3]

The new job challenged Louise's ability to foster cooperation between employers and workers. Labor militancy had grown during the post-war period. In 1919, more than four million employees in a wide range of fields participated in a total of 2,600 strikes throughout the country. The silk industry in particular had a history of considerable unrest. The introduction of heavy, double-tier looms around the turn of the century had increased production but reduced wages. In 1913, a strike by silk workers in New Jersey, Pennsylvania, and New York shut down much of the industry for three months but ultimately resulted in defeat for the unions. According to Steve Golin's book about the event, the struggle continued: "Militant weavers contested manufacturers for control over both the rate of technological change and the distribution of benefits. Especially in ribbon weaving, their fight was not hopeless because they knew that their skills remained an essential part of the productive process."[4]

Trained in Europe before emigrating to America, "the ribbon weavers had brought with them to the modern mill a tradition of craft pride and independence and a sense of their rights as artisans and as citizens. Much of the aggressiveness of Paterson's labor movement and its growing orientation toward power in the shop and the nation was a result of the influence of these skilled weavers." Their dominant ideology was socialism, but they also had "long democratic traditions. They were used to debating issues at length, listening to heretical views, exploring terms of a possible compromise, and using a secret ballot to achieve a realistic sense of the group."[5] Those traditions offered opportunities as well as challenges to a personnel manager charged with reconciling the interests of workers and employers.

American silk production had a boom year in 1919, especially silk ribbons, which were relatively inexpensive ways to accessorize or update outfits, used to an extent hard to imagine 100 years later. Yards of ribbon trimmed women's hats, skirts, sleeves, chemises, and petticoats, and little girls wore sashes and matching hair ribbons, both tied into enormous bows. Specialty stores sold lengths and rolls of ribbon as well as elaborate silk blossoms to adorn lapels or hairstyles and decorate gift baskets, boxes, and picture frames.[6] The 1934 article about Louise in the alumnae journal mentioned Smith & Kaufmann's "progressive silk ribbon factory on West 132nd Street ... often visited by earnest young students from Barnard," who were attracted not only by the product but by the company's reputation as an enlightened employer. During the 1913 strike, the owners had agreed to a nine-hour day, inspiring other ribbon weavers to abandon their demand for eight hours and seek a nine-hour settlement on a shop-by-shop basis.[7] The fact that the firm created the position of personnel manager indicated that it was committed to employee welfare.

As an industrial investigator Louise had observed how even modest improvements in working conditions increased productivity and thus benefited employers as well as workers. Her new job gave her an opportunity to put such ideas into practice. Her excitement about that prospect and about personnel management as a career for women is evident in a talk she gave to Barnard students at a vocational conference in March 1920, three months after she started the job. She described her work in a humorous, self-deprecating tone appropriate to her audience (employment managers have to "keep their fingers on the pulse of labor in an industry and administer soothing syrup or dynamite as the occasion demands"), but her list of qualifications for the position emphasized its complexity. They include "a certain amount of leadership, a knowledge of the technique of the industry, teaching ability, tact, and above all the ability to do detailed work." Fortunately, she added, "such a position pays well."[8] (The field of what is now called human resources has indeed provided access to management for women, who continue to dominate the profession. In 2016, according to the

U.S. Bureau of Labor Statistics, 72 percent of HR managers were women.)

Immediately after Louise's appearance at Barnard, an event occurred that would test her use of the skills she described. On March 8, 1920, the Amalgamated Textile Workers of America called a strike of 500 silk ribbon workers at four New York plants, including Smith & Kaufmann, demanding the abolition of piece work and the standardization of wages. The union timed the strike for a period when production of silk ribbons would normally be high in preparation for the increased demand during the spring, pressuring manufacturers to settle in order to avoid significant financial loss. As personnel manager Louise was in the forefront of efforts to end the strike by facilitating discussions among the interested parties and drafting a collective bargaining agreement that would lay the foundation for continuing co-operation. On April 9, the Greater New York locals of the "Amalgamated" called a meeting, which accepted the arbitration plan in a secret ballot with a vote of 292 for and 27 against. (The meeting took place at a location familiar to Louise: the marble-clad skyscraper at 31 Union Square that had housed the Committee on Women's Work offices until the move to the Russell Sage building on East 22nd Street.) The next day the representatives of the unions as well as the employers and the weavers at the four shops affected by the strike signed the agreement.

The U.S. Department of Labor described the agreement as "the only ... experiment providing formal machinery for collective bargaining which has been attempted in the textile industry." The provisions of the contract "relative to production and the restriction of output [were] unusual," and the Labor Department found "noteworthy" the combination of "the time and piece rate systems," which assured the worker "a fixed minimum income with the opportunity to earn more."[9] The authors of the plan, however, recognized that their approach would meet resistance from the industry. Proud of having facilitated the settlement, Louise sent a copy of the document to Mary Van Kleeck, but her cover letter implies that ultimate success was not assured: "Already other manufacturers in the industry are attacking the manufacturers who were party to the agreement, and there is going to be a lot of fight, I fear, before all is over."[10]

The agreement established shop committees, price committees, and a trade council including employers and weavers, which acted as a legislative body, approving budgets and setting trade policy, and, significantly, created the position of the impartial chairman, responsible for interpreting the contract, applying its principles to new issues, and settling disputes between management and weavers. His decision was final, and his powers and responsibilities, according to the Labor Department Bulletin, were "tremendous. He was called upon to exercise the knowledge of a technician, the wisdom of a judge, and the tact of a diplomat. He was arbitrator, judge, supreme court, and administrator of the law as set down in the agreement."[11]

For that important position, Louise told Van Kleeck, "we have secured Charles Barnes," who had been her boss as commissioner of the New York State Employment Services and had subsequently served as impartial chairman to the clothing industry in Cleveland. In a 1921 interview with the *Silk Ribbon Journal*, Barnes underscored his commitment to the position. He believed that the trade council over which he presided served an essential function: "In the discussions at the meetings of the trade council, and in the hearing of cases, the employers ... get a better understanding of the attitude of the employees and a fuller realization of their difficulties ... The employees, on their part, get an understanding of the difficulties which the employer encounters in carrying on his business." He emphasized that the approach "recognizes the human factor and ... is a real form of representative government" and commended the four silk manufacturers for their willingness to be pioneers: "It takes courage to step out of the beaten track, and both sides know they are as yet looked at askance, on the one side by their competitors, and on the other by their fellow workers, who have not at this time acquired their broadened outlook."[12]

Louise shared Barnes' vision and commitment. She had enjoyed being a pioneer as industrial researcher and as head of a public employment bureau. Now she recognized a new challenge, which she described in an article in *The American Silk Journal*: being "the one person in the management ... who understands the principles of the work, the technique, the work requirements, and the labor policies of the organization."[13] While Barnes and the Trade Council had the final word, Louise was responsible for working out the details of a permanent wage agreement to replace the accord signed in April, which provided only a temporary wage increase "effective until a thorough investigation and study could be made of the scientific basis upon which to regulate compensation."[14] To that end, she visited workshops, crowded with large, noisy looms (she included a picture of a loom among her papers to show just how big and complex it was), interviewed workers and "forepeople" (her preferred term, which recognized that "foremen" were female as well as male), and gained their trust.

From her visits to the workshops, Louise acquired the technical knowledge about silk production that she needed to do her job. She learned about "lignes," warps, trams, reeds and picks, and about the capacities of different types of looms. (Ribbon width is measured in "lignes." A "ligne" is the equivalent of 0.088 American inches; several ribbons were woven simultaneously on each loom; "ligneage" is a multiple of the width of each ribbon and the number of ribbons woven on a loom.[15]) She had to determine whether it was more demanding for a worker to weave a "ligneage" of 1,200 on two looms or a "ligneage" of 2,000 on a single loom. And she had to figure out how to define the "normal" output for a weaver given the many variables that affected it—his or her skill and training as well as the quality of the equipment and the raw material.

Interacting with weavers, Louise learned to see them "not as a mechanical automatic part of the productive machinery, but as individuals who may have the range of human likes and dislikes, weaknesses and possibilities, who can be reasoned with, interested, and with whom adjustments can be made." Her goal as personnel manager, she wrote in a 1921 article, was to develop and implement an agreement that achieved "the maximum necessary production with a minimum of effort and friction." In order to reach that goal, she needed to maintain the confidence of both management and workers through "fairness, open-mindedness and readiness to listen to both sides of any story."[16]

Louise worked with the trade council to develop the structures through which the agreement would be implemented. Included among her papers at the Schlesinger Library are several booklets outlining employee benefits such as sick leave after one month of employment, two weeks (!) of leave for "pregnancy or confinement," and a Mutual Benefit Association providing funds to be used in case of illness, accident and death. The most important of the booklets is the one describing the apprenticeship program. Before the war, the American silk industry had relied on immigrants trained in Europe; dwindling immigration necessitated the training of native-born workers, and both employers and employees, the plan insisted, shared that responsibility. From her experience with preparing women for war-time industrial work through "vestibule schools," Louise knew that defining procedures for the training of workers was essential. The plan that she drew up for Smith & Kaufmann included detailed instructions for a three-year apprentice program, such as criteria for admission (good eyesight and the ability "to read English and figure sufficiently to understand directions and keep records"), and identified specific skills to be taught, wages during training, and the members of the final examination board. The Labor Department Bulletin cited the apprenticeship plan as "one of the most worth-while accomplishments of this experiment in industrial relations," adding that "it is not a usual thing for employers and workmen to work out together problems which affect the future of an industry, but this group of manufacturers and weavers in New York City proved that such cooperation is entirely practicable."[17]

As a result of Louise's careful attention to details and ability to maintain the trust of both workers and employers, the agreement worked well for Smith & Kaufmann. The Labor Department study, which does not identify by name the four shops that signed the original on April 1920, mentions that in one of them, "the decisions of the impartial chairman were apparently carried out in spirit as well as in letter, with the result that the management, in the beginning much opposed to the idea of collective bargaining, was converted to its benefits, and the workers who voted ... voted 100% for the continuation of the plan."[18] In the *Silk Ribbon Journal* article cited above, Louise emphasized that investing in personnel management and employee benefits made sound business sense, citing a silk ribbon mill (obviously Smith & Kaufmann), which saw a decline in labor turnover from 140 percent in 1918 to 61 percent in 1920 after hiring an employment manager and saved at least

$6,000 annually—not counting additional savings from improved employee morale.[19]

The success of the agreement with the New York ribbon weavers generated a new challenge, however. In June 1921, the weavers at Smith & Kaufmann's broad silk mill in Paterson left their union and attempted to deal with the management through a shop committee. Both sides, however, knew that they needed to work out the details, and, as a result, Louise spent a busy summer investigating other plans, discussing options with both parties, and drawing up an agreement, which was signed on August 3. A trade journal reproduced the whole text in its October issue and commented that it "appears to be simple and practical," will "form a good working model for other similar plants, and may be studied with profit by all employers in similar lines. It is of especial interest at this particular time and will be watched with great attention by all employers of labor, even those outside the silk industry."[20]

For Louise, reaching agreement was a matter of applying common sense—as in the title of an article she wrote in June 1921 for *The Metropolis*, a New York weekly paper: "Common Sense in Industry—How Silk Ribbons are Manufactured without Strikes or Lockouts." The article describes for a popular audience how the collective bargaining machinery works, based on the principle "that all problems of wages and working conditions are the mutual concern of both capital and labor, and should be decided ... with full regards to the welfare of both."[21] Articles and advertisements in the *American Silk Journal* and other trade publications suggest growing acceptance of the idea that employee welfare was essential to the success of an industry. Once considered an option, embraced by some employers for philanthropic reasons, concern for working conditions and the well-being of employees had become an economic necessity in just a few years.

Few of the establishments that Louise had investigated for the Russell Sage Foundation before the war had lunch rooms, but ads in the 1921 *Silk Journal* promoted them. One used the language of scientific management ("If you want efficiency, install a lunch room"); another stressed that the cost of a "modern" cafeteria table was less than that of losing a dissatisfied employee and training a new one. An article by an industry spokesman stated that "executives are beginning to realize that a hot, palatable meal makes employees more contented, more valuable and healthy than the cold undigestible food packed in a tin box." An advertisement for air-conditioning systems promised to provide correct temperature and humidity essential to the finest quality of goods, and make "the air in the mill more healthful for the workers to breathe." In 1912, women workers had complained that their employers charged five cents every two weeks for ice water. Nine years later, a trade journal ad featured the "Vertico-Slant" drinking fountain, which "provides no resting place for bacteria; there can be no efficiency where there is disease. The employer must provide every safety guard if he wants the best service from his employees." (In the aftermath of the influenza epidemic, that message must have commanded attention!) Disregard of fire hazards had caused the Triangle Fire. A Westinghouse ad showed an attractive young lady in a Gibson blouse operating a "superior electric switch—a sound, common-sense, dependable product—the result of a humane and economical demand for safety. You cannot afford to ignore the welfare of your employees. Nor can you overlook the economy of a lower insurance rate."[22] These advertisements indicates that, while the country might have turned away from reform, the Progressive movement's efforts to transform the American workplace had a lasting impact.

European Contacts

By the spring of 1922, things appeared to be running smoothly at Smith & Kaufmann, and Louise was able to take a trip to Europe with her sister Tulla. In June, they sailed for Antwerp onboard the SS Finland, recently de-commissioned as a troop transport ship for the United States Army. Neither of them had visited Europe since the family trip to Scandinavia in 1899. They planned to tour several countries on the Continent, but, before they could do so, Louise had a professional commitment: attending a conference on industrial welfare work with more than fifty delegates from eleven countries. She was the only American participating in the event.

The site of the conference was the Château d'Argeronne in Normandy, the home of Renée de Montmort, who co-sponsored the event with the Welfare Workers' Institute of Great Britain and personally welcomed and introduced the delegates at the opening on July 2. She was fluent in English, having spent several years as a resident of a London settlement house before returning to France, where she trained as a hospital nurse and, during World War I, established a school for female factory superintendents to meet the needs of French women workers in armament and munitions plants. At Argeronne, she had hosted gatherings of literary figures and international aid workers engaged in war relief, as well as the first international Girl Scout camp. (She had founded the French Girl Scouts.)

The *château*, a seventeenth-century building, overlooked a wide lawn bordered by clusters of old trees and beds of blooming roses. Large, high-ceilinged salons, cool even on hot summer days, provided an elegant venue for presentations, discussions, and receptions. Between sessions, participants could stroll in the sixty-acre park, share insights and get to know each other. In her article about the conference, Louise described the atmosphere as "informal and unofficial" and emphasized the opportunities for "full discussion of the aims and methods of personnel work."[23]

Louise was excited to meet international colleagues who shared the principles that had informed her career and were finding ways to humanize work while increasing efficiency in the factories of their countries. Her contribution to the conference was an address on "Personnel Work in America," which was re-printed in the August issue of the *Personnel Administration* journal. She had been asked to speak on "Welfare Work in America" but insisted on changing the title because of the evolution of the profession and the paternalistic connotations of the term "welfare," which workers and union leaders distrusted as an attempt to dissuade them from organizing to seek improvements in wages and hours. Also, she claimed, "the community" was assuming responsibility "for all matters relating to health, recreation and education ... and the opportunities for receiving such service should not be dependent upon a person's continuing in the employ of a particular plant." Qualifying this optimistic assumption, she acknowledged the necessity of "stimulating public efforts to provide such services"; she also emphasized that "the actual experiences of welfare workers are an important asset in working out methods."[24]

The tendency, Louise knew from her own experience at Smith & Kaufmann, was "for personnel workers more and more to get into the production end … concerning themselves with questions of training, promotions, job analysis, time studies … wages and production standards, working hours and regularity of production." Their principal concern, however, was "the human factor"—the employee in relation to his job—and their profession required "a deep understanding of human nature and reactions and experience in dealing with men and women, whether they be the workers, or the plant foremen, or executives or the employer himself!" Quoting "a successful employment manager of a large firm in New York [who] once said that she felt that her whole life had been a training school for her present job," she might have been speaking of herself.[25]

At the end of the event, Louise reported in an article published by *The Survey* in August 1922, delegates agreed that the mission of personnel work was to enable industry to "render the best service to the community, with the least effort and cost" and to "conserve and develop in industrial life the spiritual, mental and physical well-being of all who share in rendering this service." To carry out that mission, they decided to meet again in Holland two years later "for the purpose of forming an international organization."[26] Louise served on the provisional committee charged with implementing the resolutions adopted at the Argeronne conference and drawing up plans for the organization that would become the International Industrial Relations Institute, known as the IRI. Other professional journals beside *The Survey* reported on the conference, and the *Daily News* covered the event in an August 8th article under the headline "Miss Odencrantz will return from Europe in September."

After submitting her article to *The Survey*, Louise was free to enjoy a long holiday with her sister. The two of them spent the rest of the summer touring France, Italy, and Switzerland, benefitting from a favorable currency exchange rate that enabled them to afford hotels, meals, and an occasional glass of wine—an unfamiliar treat to somebody living in Prohibition-era America. No letters describing their experience have survived, but Louise painted water colors of some of the sites they visited, which are surprisingly accomplished considering that she had no artistic training. She observed and recorded the visual features with the same attention to detail that she used as an industrial investigator.

Promoting the Human Factor

The exchange of ideas with European colleagues had strengthened Louise's commitment to the alliance between industry and social work promoted by the Taylor Society, of which she had become a member, and to whom she reported on the conference. She also joined Mary Van Kleeck, Frances Perkins, and Molly Dewson (a leader in the National Consumers' League, who would later head the Democratic National Committee's Women's Division and serve on the Social Security Board) on a committee charged with defining industrial social work as a profession. They considered adopting the term "social engineering" but rejected it as inaccurate and confusing.[27]

Louise, however, found the engineering analogy useful when addressing industry audiences. Speaking to the New Haven Industrial Relations Council in October 1922, she called the personnel manager the "human engineer," whose place in the organization is as important as that of the mechanical engineer: "His whole business is to increase production through his management of the human element, just as the master mechanic improves it by keeping the machines in order." Managing the human element, however, required a different approach than mechanical engineering: "Industry can succeed only if it is a living organism of which the men and women workers form a conscious part. Industry must recognize that the essential parts are not automatic, but human beings with minds and souls, with tremendous possibilities and serious weaknesses, likes and dislikes, but above all with a latent power of self-action, which is the greatest power in industry." The task of the personnel manager is to release that energy and "to promote the wider usefulness of the human element in production through necessary readjustments of the work, the worker and his surroundings, and at the same time to render the worker a conscious and interested part of the organization."[28]

Improving "the industrial welfare of workers" would not only achieve "better and more efficient management in industry" but strengthen the whole fabric of society, Louise told the National Conference of Social Work in May 1923. "The job is the hub of [the worker's] industrial life—his means of livelihood; and it ought to be his joy and his incentive for thought, action and interest. It is his chief basis of relationship and contact with his fellow workers." If all workers had "suitable and satisfying [jobs] …some at least of our economic and social problems would diminish or disappear."[29] The speech appeared as a lead article in *The Public Health Nurse* a few months later, suggesting the appeal of these ideas to audiences beyond industry.

Defeat

The idea that effective personnel management would create industrial harmony was gaining wide acceptance, but, as Louise was about to discover, the very success of the cooperation efforts she spearheaded could generate problems. She had helped her employer weather the challenges of the 1920-21 economic downturn, and 1922 was a year of consolidation for the American economy, which re-gained full employment by 1923. Market conditions for the silk industry also improved, but workers' confidence that the recovery placed them in a stronger position created a new challenge for the collective bargaining process.

A small militant group in the union, whose economic philosophy opposed all compromises with employers, objected to being bound by the agreement and wished to be free to negotiate for wage increases at a time of increased demand for silk. In June, matters reached a head. The executive board of the union, in a letter addressed to "Dear Comrade" and signed "Fraternally yours," called all members to a meeting on June 14th, emphasizing that "this a very important question, and every member should be present, those who wish to continue the present system and those who are opposed to it." Only 156 showed up. The Labor Department attributed failure to attend the meeting "to apathy on the part of the more conservative weavers, who felt either too sure that the result would be favorable to the collective bargaining plan or who were indifferent as to its outcome." Most of the workers attending were opposed to the agreement. 96 voted to abrogate it while 60 voted against the motion.[30]

The Labor Department account of the abrogation does not mention any names (although it is likely that Louise was the source of some of the information), and there is no reference there or elsewhere to her reaction. She must have been disappointed in the outcome and concerned about the loss of Charles Barnes, the impartial chairman, whose salary was paid by union dues. Carrying on without him would be a challenge, but it seems that the silk-ribbon-weavers continued to operate under a shop arrangement like the one Smith & Kaufmann had with the broad-silk weavers in Paterson and that she still handled the functions of personnel management.

The 1923 improvement in the silk industry's prospects turned out to be short-lived. The American silk industry had been the largest in the world at the beginning of the twentieth century, thanks to its application of mechanized processes to what elsewhere was still largely a handcraft. The success led to overproduction, which, in combination with the competition from artificial fibers (rayon) and changing consumer preferences, caused the decline of the industry beginning in the mid-twenties. An early example of this trend, Smith & Kaufmann closed its doors permanently in 1924.

Louise refers briefly to the company's liquidation in her work resumé, but there is no record of her reaction. One imagines that she was deeply disappointed after five years of trying to prove that cooperation between workers and management and recognition of their shared interests would produce positive outcomes. And she must have thought about the weavers and "forepeople" for whom their job had been their "means of livelihood" as well as their "chief basis of relationship and contact with … fellow workers." She was probably exhausted as well and did not immediately look for another job but traveled abroad for most of the following year.

Chapter X

Life Choices and Relationships

Independence

On February 25, 1925, Louise sailed for Europe, planning to visit several countries on the Continent and in North Africa before attending the conference in Holland that formally established the IRI. From Algiers, she sent a photo to her family with the following note on the back: "How do you like me in an Arab wedding costume which I put on in an Arab house in [name of town illegible]?" The photo reflects her interest in traditional clothing as reflective of culture, which led her to collect dolls wearing local dress throughout her travels. The costume was a tourist prop, and she knew her mother would appreciate the theatrical flourish, but it is also possible to see the photo and note as a humorously defiant gesture, acknowledging that this was as close to getting married as she was likely to come. Her papers leave no trace of her social life, and there is no way of telling whether she made a deliberate choice to focus on her career or was simply too busy to consider relationships that might distract her from her work. At any rate, by the age of forty, she had held a number of responsible jobs and earned enough money to be able to pay for several months of travel.

Staying single was not unusual for women of Louise's generation. Pauline Goldmark saw Francis Perkins' marriage "as a defection from the social work movement" according to Kristin Downey's biography. Pauline and her sister Josephine "had busy activist careers; their equally intelligent sister Alice, married to a Boston lawyer named Louis Brandeis, had largely retreated from public view."[1] Of twenty-eight women that Susan Ware profiles in her book *Beyond Suffrage: Women in the New Deal,* ten never married. She cites Sue Shelton White, who wrote in *The Nation,* "Marriage is too much of a compromise; it lops off a woman's life as an individual."[2]

Frederikke probably supported her daughter's decision to focus on her career although she herself was happily married to a loyal and supportive husband and seems to have maintained a strong sense of her personal identity. It was to a large extent through her efforts—as a music teacher in Houston and New York, and, later, through her shrewd financial investments—that the family maintained a solid middle-class life. But a letter to Marguerite, written in 1928 when Louise was again travelling in Europe, suggests that she envied her daughter's independence: "We have had several letters from Louise who seems to have a great time. This is the century for unmarried people, who never get too old for pleasure, and why should they?" She also commented on the recent death of her niece Marianne's husband: "There she is now with 2 children and I suppose very little money, she might earn some by her painting but it will be hard; she had a very fine husband they all say. The best die I suppose. They, most men or some of them, only care to marry if they can get a free housekeeper; they do not care for a family."[3] Marianne (who was my grandmother) did face a struggle providing for her two children after my grandfather's death, but the comment hardly reflects Frederikke's own experience; Gustaf was by all accounts a devoted husband and father.

Indeed, Frederikke's own marriage gave her considerable independence, financial and otherwise. Gustaf appeared to have relied on her and deferred to her. In September 1930, he wrote to Marguerite from the farm in New Jersey, where he and Frederikke spent their summers, that "here is quiet, no visitors and not many passing neither. Piano is now on the bum again—too damp for it. When we are going in is uncertain. Ma likes to stay here for a while, but I don't care to stay much longer than this month—it commences to be dreary in the night."[4] The implication is that "Ma" made the decisions while he might grumble but went along.

Frederikke also took charge of the family's finances. According to Marguerite, her brother Fred's first job with a subsidiary of U.S. Steel allowed him to buy company stock as part of his compensation. That inspired his mother to invest in shares, and apparently her portfolio survived or recovered from the Depression. Her last will, probated after her death in 1939, stated that "To my dear husband Gustaf I will the interest during his lifetime from all of my cash money and securities. To my husband I also will during his lifetime the income from all my real estate or the income from the money if sold."[5] (It is not clear whether the will referred to the Nebraska homestead and the land in Texas or to other property.) Louise's observation of her parents' marriage would have shown her that it was possible for a wife to stay in charge, but perhaps she also sensed that there were things her mother would have liked to do but was not able to because of her responsibility for Gustaf and the family.

Relationships

One of the benefits of remaining single was the opportunity to build significant personal and professional relationships with other women. Susan Ware points out that "the outstanding characteristic of women's participation in the New Deal was the development of a network of friendship and cooperation among the women, which maximized their influence in politics and government."[6]

During the 1920s, New York City became a center of national leadership for the social welfare movement, and the concentration of organizational headquarters in an area near Gramercy Park facilitated interaction among its leaders. Two iconic buildings were on East 22nd Street: the United Charities Building at #105, whose tenants included the National Consumers' League, the National Child Labor Committee, and the New York School of Philanthropy, and, across the street at #120, the Russell Sage Foundation headquarters, which also housed other social-service organizations, such as the American Association of Social Workers and the Library of Social Work. Florence Kelley, Josephine Goldmark, and Frances Perkins had their offices in the former building, and Mary Van Kleeck and Pauline Goldmark in the latter.

It was a small world, Perkins commented: "Somebody introduced you to somebody in the elevator, said who you were, and so you became acquainted ... You knew everybody else that was operating. It was a small and sort of integrated professional world as there weren't so many of them. Mutual help and fairness prevailed, and I remember it to this day." Friendship and trust developed among these women, who "thought of themselves as part of a large family bound together by an almost mystical commitment to social reform."[7]

Even when her jobs took her to other parts of the city, Louise maintained her connection to this network, especially to Mary Van Kleeck, with whom she shared her efforts to implement their common ideas and principles in her work as employment office director and personnel manager. In her diary, Van Kleeck listed a conference with Miss Odencrantz scheduled for March 2, 1917, noting that she had cancelled all other appointments. But, although the two of them worked together for decades and had deep respect for each other, they continued to address each other formally—at least in writing—perhaps because that was standard behavior at the time. Louise broke the code once, beginning a December 8, 1920 letter, in which she sought advice about the apprentice training program she was developing for Smith & Kaufmann, "My Dear Mary." Van Kleeck's response, dated two weeks later, began "My Dear Miss Odencrantz," recommended consulting the Executive Director of the Taylor Society, who might "secure introductions to some of the plants where attention has been given to job analysis as a basis for training," and concluded "With the season's greetings, sincerely yours, Mary Van Kleeck." Despite the implicit rebuke (which might reflect Van Kleeck's personality, described by contemporaries as dignified, reserved, and "without warmth"[8]), Louise remained cordial. To a subsequent letter, after Commerce Secretary Herbert Hoover had invited Van Kleeck to join the President's Conference on Unemployment, she added "Congratulations on your appointment to the Unemployment Conference—they need you. Best wishes for good results."[9] The two continued to work together on Russell Sage projects and in the Taylor Society and the IRI throughout the 1920s although they did not always agree.

Other relationships were more casual. Among the papers she deposited with the Schlesinger Library, Louise included the following notice from the April 1929 *Survey* "Gossip" column, which suggests that she and her friends mixed seriousness and fun: "Five handsome young women appeared together at the Grand Central bound for a week-end at the Caroline Country Club—and four of the five had it. ... 'Had what?' you ask. 'Surely not—Wrong again. They each had a copy of the German issue of Survey Graphic, and Louise Odencrantz, who was one of those who had it, said they almost had their picture taken for Gossip."[10] (Was Louise pleased that, at the age of 45, she was included in a group of "handsome young women"?)

Genuine, long-lasting friendships also grew out of professional connections. Louise first encountered Ruth Reticker, University of Chicago Class of 1912, at a Taylor Society conference. Their professional paths crossed again during the 1930s, when both were involved in implementing New Deal unemployment policies. They visited each other regularly in Washington, where Ruth lived, or in New York, and, in 1956, they travelled to Scandinavia together. Ruth had a successful civil service career, but, in a letter announcing her retirement, she downplayed her professional achievements and emphasized the role of friendship in her life: "I've failed to realize [my] youthful dreams of a 'career' and fame, but there have been compensations in working on worthwhile causes and making friends along the way."[11] Louise never mentioned dreams of career and fame, but she would agree about the value of friendships and "working on worthwhile causes."

Like many single women of her generation, Louise shared a home with sisters or friends and never lived alone. After the Odencrantz children had finished their education and got jobs, Gustaf and Frederikke gave up their home in New York and lived year-round on the farm in New Jersey for some years. The four siblings rented several successive apartments, moving every year in search of better accommodations. Marguerite gave the reasons in the following list, which suggests the young people's improving earnings—and changes in the New York housing market:

1. We wanted outside rooms, instead of our former railroad flat.
2. We wanted heat and hot water.
3. We each wanted our own room.
4. We wanted to live in the Bronx; so many of our friends had moved up there.

5. We wanted to live in a rooming house with no responsibility.
6. We wanted to have our meals in and moved to a boarding house.
7. We wanted to housekeep again, so we could entertain our friends.
8. We wanted one less room because our brother had married.
9. We wanted to live in an elevator apartment.
10. We wanted a doorman.[12]

After Marguerite married in 1923, Tulla and Louise continued to room together in New York City until Tulla took a position in Albany and moved there during the 1930s.

Did Louise ever consider marriage? Was she ever in love? There is no way of answering those questions. As Susan Ware comments, the women of her generation "consciously separated their personal from their professional lives [and] might not have foreseen that future generations would be interested in their personal lives. Just as likely, the women chose not to share the tensions and rewards of this side of their lives with posterity."[13]

International Network

Louise's contacts with women in other countries were particularly important to her. Since her return from Normandy in 1922, she had been working with other participants in that first meeting to draw up plans for another conference. In June 1925, at the end of her European tour, she joined other "welfare" and personnel specialists in Vlissingen (Flushing), Holland, for an event that launched the International Industrial Relations Institute, the IRI.

Dutch labor historian Ruth Oldenziel has traced the evolution of the organization: "The women who banded together in the IRI tried to fashion an alternative to the post-war political climate. Like the ILO [the International Labor Organization], the IRI sought an advisory and non-governmental role in the spirit of the progressive tradition, believing that exposure of the facts provided the most powerful tool in educating and persuading the public to sup-

Louise was in her forties when this photo was taken.

port far-reaching reforms." Applying the principles of scientific management, "the IRI sought to improve working conditions and resolve conflicts between labor and capital primarily through research and discussion ... care, welfare, and dialogue figured as key words." The 1925 Conference elected Kerstin Hesselgren, the first female member of Sweden's parliament, president of the organization, and chose three vice-presidents: Renée de Montmort of France (who had hosted the first conference of what became the IRI at her Normandy estate), Louise Odencrantz, and Cees van der Leeuw, a multitalented Dutch industrialist whose factory eventually became a UNESCO world heritage site.[14]

Membership expanded from the less-than-sixty people that had gathered in Normandy to about 300, still predominantly female although male participants also joined. At the Vlissingen conference, a panel on employee representation featured Samuel Lewisohn, a prominent New York industrialist, financier, and philanthropist, Gustav Dabringhaus, "*Betriebsrat*" (employee representative) at the Krupp Steelworks, and Dorothy Cadbury, director of the British chocolate factory that her family had founded. Dutch "Efficiency Engineer" Ernst Hymans gave a presentation on "Employment Management as a Condition of and Means to Efficiency," and Louise led the discussion that followed. In her report on the conference, she quoted his statement, with which she agreed: "Real scientific management which considers the human element as well as the methods and machines is, after all, one of the fundamental methods of improving human welfare in industry not alone in the provision of proper physical conditions but in the establishment of fair and just methods and relations, independent of the prejudices and personalities of supervisors."[15]

For Americans, disappointed that their country had turned isolationist and did not participate in the League of Nations or in most other forms of international cooperation, the IRI provided a venue to meet colleagues from Europe and Asia. Even after her career took her into fields not directly related to personnel work, Louise continued to attend planning meetings in the U.S. and participated in conferences. She chaired a roundtable on "Policies in Employment and Discharge" at a congress held at Girton College, Cambridge, in 1928 and published articles on the event, in which she emphasized the diversity of experiences that participants brought as well as their shared perceptions: "One is impressed with the extent to which the particular conditions of a country modify and influence the development and application of a general principle to meet its own needs. On the other hand, one is equally impressed with certain universal tendencies, both in practice and in basic principles of industrial relations."[16] Her files at the Schlesinger Archives contain a call for the 1931 Congress in Amsterdam, which she probably attended, but she did not report on it.

It is noteworthy that a small and obscure organization—headed by women—was able to attract participants, male as well as female, who had or would go on to distinguished careers. They addressed issues of importance for all workers, but, Oldenziel insists, "women reformers and those linked to women's labor issues played such a crucial role in its establishment that it could be characterized as a women's organization."[17] As such, it offered opportunities for women to learn from and support each other as they looked for ways to develop professionally and to influence the agenda in their respective countries. That influence may have lasted, but the organization lost funding and reduced activities during the 1930s and, when World War II started, it shut down.

Chapter XI

Moving in New Directions

Analyzing Social Work

As personnel manager, Louise had brought the perspective of social work to industry. On her return from Europe in 1925, she reversed the process by applying the job analysis method of scientific management to the field of social work in a "job study" commissioned by the American Association of Social Workers (AASW) and funded by the Russell Sage Foundation, which also provided office space for the AASW in its building on 22nd Street. Once again, she worked with Mary van Kleeck to implement ideas that the latter had articulated and that the two of them probably discussed. In a 1922 article entitled "The Professional Organization of Social Work," Van Kleeck had emphasized the need for the profession to focus on "practical activity and methods which can be tested by results" and to function "as a group in conscious recognition of its relations with other professions."[1] Louise had never been a social worker, but she was able to apply to that field her experience in analyzing relationships between employees and organizations and between individuals and their assigned tasks.

After working in other parts of New York City for more than a decade, Louise was back at the Russell Sage building on 22nd Street, in the neighborhood that was home to organizations carrying on the ideas of the Progressive movement. There she had access to a research library, considered "the best place in the country for the study of practical problems related to poverty, social service agencies and public health,"[2] not only because of its contents but because of the setting: a beautiful double-height space on the eighth and ninth floors with leather doors, marble floors, and leaded-glass windows. Preparing for her study, she immersed herself in the materials available there, including the AASW's pamphlets and vocational analyses of nationally distributed questionnaires and studies of social work published by the Foundation.

The Russell Sage Foundation's core mission, "the improvement of social and living conditions in the United States," included the professionalization of social work. In 1910, it had recruited Mary Richmond to serve as head of its Charity Organization Department. Her biographer, Ellen Agnew, calls her "an important leader, teacher, and practical theorist in ... the transition from nineteenth-century practices of voluntary charity to twentieth-century professional social work."[3] Her textbook *Social Diagnosis* (1917), which went through five editions in two years, defined case work as the core function of social work. She insisted that "social reform and social casework must of necessity progress together." Caseworkers must identify the surrounding economic and social problems as well as individual issues, and intervention may require changing the environment as well as enabling the client to cope with it.[4]

That dual perspective was familiar to Louise from her settlement experience, which had taught her to respect individuals' efforts to take charge of their lives and to identify the circumstances that prevented them from doing so. She mentioned Richmond's work several times in her own study and included it in a list of essential books for the social worker's library, but she was probably unable to consult the author while doing her research because declining health prevented Richmond from working at the Foundation office; she died in 1928.

Louise's book, *The Social Worker in Family, Medical and Psychiatric Social Work,* builds on the vision of Richmond and other pioneers, but her approach reflects the changes that were affecting the profession during the 1920s. For Richmond, social work was "akin to a religious calling," whose practitioners "would dedicate themselves to personal service and to the development of an inner center of personal meaning, both in themselves and in the individuals and families they were assisting."[5] During the post-war period, however, as city agencies consolidated social services into larger structures, the emphasis shifted toward rationalization and "specialized assignments with supervision, casework procedures and standardized report forms" according to historian Daniel Walkowitz. As a result, "social workers found their professional autonomy limited by austere and routinized working conditions in new bureaucracies."[6] Louise's study, however, emphasized the essential contributions of the individual employee. Her experience in industry had taught her the importance of considering the human element as well as methods and tools.

The introduction to the book acknowledged the difficulties of applying job analysis to social work. In industry, the method "has served as a basis for determining the necessary qualifications for a position ... evolving training methods, [and] for salary grading and organized methods of promotion." The field of social work, however, "deals with such intangible things as human relationships in a field where there exist practically no methods of measuring results. ... The person who fills the job is a factor in determining its content, nature and conditions, [and] content and objectives are modified by the interpretation of the individual worker." Although no general outline would apply to all positions, the study would try "to picture the most usual practices and conditions, and at the same time to point out variations which ... indicate experiments and the trend of development."[7]

In order to capture the perspectives of social workers, Louise conducted field research in New York, Boston, and Philadelphia, interviewing "individuals who were engaged in the job analyzed, those responsible for its organization and supervision, and others ... who were in contact with the work" including executives, supervisors and staff members. She observed them on the job, collected their logs of daily visits, attended staff conferences, and read case records, handbooks, and time studies. Wherever she went, she applied the interview skills that she had developed through her work for the Russell Sage Foundation and was gratified to encounter "the frankness and professional attitude with which all were ready to contribute their experience."[8] She also contacted other organizations and schools of social work.

The first section of the book concerns family social work, reflecting Mary Richmond's understanding of social work in which the Victorian ideal of the family was central.[9] This area engaged the largest number of case workers, who, although their "primary concern is for the individual," recognize "the infinite possibilities of the family for conditioning the development and the personality of its individual members." Louise's use of non-technical metaphors is interesting: "the family and its relationships are the setting for the drama of life," and "there is an art of family life."[10] Was she thinking about the "drama" of her own family's life, the challenges they had faced immigrating and moving across the country, about the "art" her parents employed to hold it all together, and about how these experiences had conditioned her own development and personality?

The second section focuses on a relatively new field: medical social work, which had only been practiced for about twenty years. Studying this group of professionals introduced Louise to the concerns of handicapped patients, a broad category that included cardiac and tubercular cases, epileptics, and people suffering loss of limb or otherwise immobilized. ("Handicapped" was still a standard term, not considered demeaning, and the word "crippled" was used in a technical sense.) The responsibilities of medical social workers were broad: "Assisting the crippled and industrially handicapped to secure vocational guidance and retraining and suitable employment, and stimulating them to find and retain employment, counteracting tendencies towards self-pity or discouragement."[11] That dimension of medical social work seems to have held special appeal for Louise; the sentence quoted describes the position she would take on after finishing the study: directing an employment center for the handicapped.

Psychiatric as distinct from medical social work was an even more recent application of the case work method. It was a direct result of World War I, which created a demand for professionals trained to consider social factors in connection with the rehabilitation of soldiers suffering from shell shock and other nervous disorders. Smith College and other institutions developed specialized training programs to meet this need. "The social worker brings to the psychiatric problem her special skills in evaluating social data and in effecting environmental adjustments," Louise wrote in her introduction to this section of the book.[12] Graduates from programs such as the one at Smith had high professional status, but there were only 300-400 of them in the whole country. Her use of the female pronoun in the sentence quoted above reflects the fact that most social workers were women. Their salaries were low, considering that most had college degrees and many had done graduate work. Promotion to a supervisory position might bring an increase, but the job study establishes a clear correlation between inadequate compensation and turnover.

Before submitting the manuscript to Harper & Row, Louise sent a draft "for detailed comments to the organizations visited and also to persons in each field to see how far it represented conditions throughout the country. The criticism of these persons was considered and incorporated in the final revision."[13] Reviewers recognized the value of including field workers' perspective on their work—and the effort it took to collect it. Mary Antoinette Cannon, Professor at Columbia's School of Social Work, congratulated the AASW on "having been able to produce through Miss Odencrantz' able workmanship so careful a piece of analysis in a field hitherto unbroken to this form of study. ... It must have cost enormous labor to achieve such clarity and simplicity in the face of a welter of complexities." The job study had achieved its objective according to another reviewer: "This work will do much towards establishing the right of social work to be considered professional. It is an authoritative statement of what social case workers consider their work to consist of." Long after its immediate relevance had expired, references to it appear; a 1983 article in *The Journal of Sociology & Social Welfare* mentions Odencrantz's "classic job analysis text," and Walkowitz, in the source quoted above, cites her "detailed 1929 study of social work."[14]

Serving the Handicapped

Observing social workers who were providing services for the handicapped made Louise aware of what was happening in that field and of how much there was to be done. The need to provide rehabilitation and job opportunities for soldiers and sailors who returned from World War I with a permanent handicap was obvious. Even before America entered the conflict, war production's increased demand for workers had caused employers to consider disabled applicants they might previously have rejected. Two acts of Congress had created and funded programs for vocational rehabilitation; the one passed in 1918 focused on veterans, and the Civilian Vocational Rehabilitation Act of 1920 extended services to the wider population. In spite of these efforts, prejudice against the handicapped was widespread at the time. According to historian Kim E. Nielsen, during the early twentieth century, Americans "with disabilities fought against increasingly stringent and harsh laws and cultural attitudes. ... Physical 'defects,' both scientists and the casual observer increasingly assumed, went hand in hand with mental and moral 'defects.'"[15] Changing this mindset was a high priority for organizations serving the handicapped.

In New York City alone, more than a dozen different agencies—some narrowly, others broadly focused—provided training and placement for people with disabilities. Those agencies were the subject of a 1927 report, *Securing Employment for the Handicapped: A Study of Placement Agencies for This Group in New York City* by Mary La Dame, a member of the Russell Sage Department of Industrial Studies. She and Louise had served together on the Executive Committee of the Clearing House for War Time Training for Women, and the fact that they both worked out of offices in the headquarters on 22nd Street enabled them to exchange ideas while doing research on related topics. (They would meet again in Washington during the 1930s, when La Dame became Associate Director for the U.S. Employment Services under Frances Perkins and Louise was a consultant to the same agency.) La Dame's report pointed out that there was considerable duplication among the various agencies and concluded that if handicapped employment "is to make much progress in winning the cooperation of the medical profession and of employers, it needs the active attention of able executives [with] administrative and promotional ability of considerable caliber."[16]

Those qualities were ones that Louise had demonstrated in her previous positions, and, when the New York Employment Center for the Handicapped opened in 1927 as a privately funded non-profit organization, she was an obvious candidate for Executive Director. She could have remained with the American Association of Social Workers and completed a second volume in the job analysis series, but, faced with a choice between another theoretical study and the opportunity to make a difference in the lives of people, she did not hesitate in choosing the latter. She held that position longer than any other—nine years—and the description of it in her work resumé suggests pride in what she achieved: "Developed new methods of procedure; did considerable research into the suitability of various kinds of work for the handicapped; did considerable writing and speaking."[17]

In 1916, Louise had told an interviewer that directing the employment bureau for women "meant the foundation of my life work."[18] Her subsequent career took turns that she had not anticipated at the time, but her approach was consistent: Get the facts, discover how they impact people's lives, bring the parties together, and find a solution that benefits everybody. Directing a public employment agency had taught her how to match client skills and needs with the demands of the market, and as personnel officer she had gained further experience in considering the point of view of management as well as that of workers. Her study of social work methodology increased her awareness of counselling strategies. She welcomed the pioneering opportunities of each position, looked at its demands, applied her previous experience, and defined the new job as a profession.

The first order of business was to identify the categories of "handicapped" that the Employment Center could serve. Louise provided the following definition in a lecture to the State Conference of Social Work in Albany in November 1929: "A person is considered eligible if he is unable to pursue or secure work in his regular employment within a reasonable length of time or if he must secure work outside his regular line on account of his handicap. It includes those whose appearance such as lameness or other disfigurement prejudices employers against taking them, and those who require supervision in their work surroundings such as those with a cardiac condition."[19]

The Center referred the blind and hard-of hearing to other specialized organizations and recognized that some handicaps were so severe that they made placement in regular industry impossible. During the first two years of operation, about 6,000 people with a wide range of disabilities registered. Orthopedic cases were the largest single group (43 percent); the rest included people suffering from heart disease, tuberculosis, hernias, gastric ulcers, and speech defects as well as some "convalescent and post-operative cases." Placement secretaries were designated for each type of handicap. Their shared aim was "to place the applicant where he can make good in spite of any disabilities and where he will not endanger himself or others." Many of the clients had little idea of the kind of work they could do; other complicating factors included age, illiteracy, lack of training and general education, inability to speak English, and work experience limited to dying trades. (Technological developments were a mixed blessing for the disabled: They benefited from "the advance of surgical medicine, improved artificial appliances, physio-therapy, electrical and other services," but increasing use of high-speed machinery, especially in larger factories, created new problems.) Despite all these challenges, during its second year of operation, the Center found positions for 1,756 men and 456 women.[20]

Outreach to employers was an important reason for the Center's success in placing clients. In her study, Mary La Dame had complained that, in their eagerness to help applicants, placement agencies "have allowed [their] need of employment to take precedence over [their] qualifications for work. This policy is extremely short-sighted, for the co-operation of employers is absolutely essential ... and can be achieved in the long run only through satisfactory service to them."[21] Louise knew that she had to get out of the office to meet prospective employers, listen to their concerns and interests, and see how their plants operated. In a speech to the American College of Surgeons in New York in 1931, she defined her role as that of an intermediary, who understood the abilities as well as the limitations of persons with physical defects, knew the requirements of individual jobs and the general requirements of industry, and could interpret one to the other: "Selling the idea of employing a handicapped person to employers is slow work and meets with constant opposition. It must be done largely on the basis of the ability and handicap of the individual applicant. Perhaps, it might rather be called a job for a high-powered salesman who knows his goods and his prospects, instead of a social worker!"[22]

Getting to know "the goods," the specific strengths and shortcomings of each person seeking help, was the focus of Louise's instructions to counselors. They should always assume that applicants had something to offer, ask them about their education, training, and experience in order to determine what occupations they were qualified to pursue, and, if the disability prevented them from continuing in their previous line of work, help them identify other skills and find alternative ways of using their experience. (The Center offered vocational guidance and training as well as placement.) Louise gave the same advice to the social workers assembled in Albany that she had given to her staff: Consider "the person himself with all his abilities, mental attitudes and limitation as well as his physical handicap"; be sensitive to "the effects of an accident upon the man's mind, a feeling of insecurity about his future, exaggeration or underestimation of his condition," but discourage him from defining himself by his disability.[23] In the manual she wrote at the end of her tenure, she again emphasized that "it is not what is gone but what is left that counts," and that clients "are people like you and me, who, even if we have developed a physical disability through an accident or illness, nevertheless retain our mentality and other abilities."[24]

Louise's regular speeches to organizations dealing with the handicapped, which were often printed in professional journals, suggest that she was an effective speaker. She described individual cases vividly and added an occasional touch of humor as exemplified by a lecture she delivered to occupational therapists in Philadelphia in 1934. Her staff had arranged for a handicapped man to sell candy from a push cart in city parks on a commission basis, and he was very satisfied: "The work was out of doors, the man was on his own, and after he had pushed his cart to his location, he could sit on a stool by his car. We used to call this our largest sheltered workshop!" Another example was that of a young woman who came to the office walking with two canes and felt no employer would accept her. "She was placed in a sheltered workshop where she found girls more disabled than herself. She did pasting, inserting, and other hand work. Three months later she had discarded one cane, was traveling alone from the other end of town, and the supervisor advised us that she must be ready for work as she was getting so 'fresh' and running around so much."[25] The examples demonstrate another reason for the Center's success: continued monitoring of individuals after placement—a need that Mary La Dame had pointed out in her report.

Emphasizing the satisfaction and cheerfulness of the two clients described above was part of Louise's effort to change perceptions of handicapped people, who, if they were acknowledged at all, were seen as objects of pity. That attitude prevails and continues to offend. In her preface to *About Us: Essays From The New York Times Disability Series,* published in 2019, Rosemarie Garland-Thomsen challenges that concept: "the most unjustified stereotype about disability is that our lives are filled with relentless and unaccountable suffering."[26] Changing this and other stereotypes was a major goal of Louise's outreach. She knew that integrating the handicapped into the workforce—and into society—depended on colleagues and other members of the public recognizing their full humanity and their contributions.

In her efforts to increase understanding, Louise emphasized that people with disabilities were not looking for charity but for ways in which they could contribute to the community. Early in her tenure, she wrote a letter to *The New York Times* asking readers to suggest work for an Italian-born former longshoreman, who had lost a leg in an accident, spoke some English, had excellent references, and was "anxious to support his wife and four children." Later, she utilized the new media of radio to remind audiences of what handicapped people had achieved. In one of her broadcasts, she asked listeners to "imagine the loss to the General Electric Company if [it] had refused to employ—because he was a cripple—a certain young man who later became known as the wizard Charles Steinmetz."[27] Steinmetz, who revolutionized industry through his use of alternating current and the development of electric motors, had almost been denied admission to the United States by immigration officers because he was a hunch-back and only four feet three inches tall.[28]

As part of her effort to reach a general audience, Louise spoke to the Rotary Club of New York in October 1930. The title given to the published version of her speech, "An Address by the Fairer Sex,"[29] underscores how hard it was at the time for a woman to be accepted strictly on her professional credentials, but the text shows her ability to relate to the Rotarian audience. She cited the examples of a boy, lame since childhood, who had completed a course in mechanical drafting and was working in the field, and another with "one arm short" who sought employment as an office boy and hoped to become a lawyer. As a result of her presentation, the Rotary Boys' Work Committee agreed to work closely with the Employment Center—an example of the supportive network that she was building.

It was not until the 1960s that advocates of disability rights formed an influential movement, and almost another thirty years before Congress passed the Americans with Disabilities Act. Central to these efforts were the same principle and goal that governed Louise's approach—recognizing the full humanity of disabled individuals and integrating them into the community. She would have understood the argument made by Rosemarie Garland-Thomsen in a 2016 article on "Becoming Disabled" (defined as developing "a sturdy disability identity"): "Becoming disabled demands learning how to live effectively as a person with disabilities, not just living as a disabled person trying to become nondisabled. It also demands the awareness and cooperation of others who don't experience these challenges. Becoming disabled means moving from isolation to community, from ignorance to knowledge about who we are, from exclusion to access, and from shame to pride."[30]

Increasingly recognized as an authority in the field of handicapped employment, Louise was asked to take on other related projects. In preparation for a November 1930 White House Conference on Children, she served on the Committee for the Physically and Mentally Handicapped and contributed to the almost 600-page long preliminary report distributed to conference participants. She saved her invitation to the event among her papers but left no record of what turned out to be a tension-filled occasion. Others did, however, among them Florence Kelley, who wrote to a friend that "every session of Mr. Hoover's child conference was worse than every other session."[31] The most contentious issue was a recommendation by a sub-committee that the medical work of the Children's Bureau be transferred to the federal Public Health Service. Opponents (including Kelley, Grace Abbott, head of the Children's Bureau, physician Alice Hamilton, and Lillian Wald, who pioneered public health nursing and founded the Henry Street Settlement in New York) argued that "different kinds of work for children could best be done by a single agency." Given Louise's concern about child labor and her support of policies that favored children's welfare, she was probably among "the array of distinguished people" who attended a meeting about the proposed transfer in "a small unventilatable hall in the ground back of the Red Cross building" with seats only for committee members. When Mary Anderson, Director of the Women's Bureau, brought a chair into the room, the head of the committee "leaped from his platform, ran to her, grabbed the chair out of her hands, [and] shouted, 'this is for a man on the committee.'"[32] After a stormy closing session held in the auditorium of Constitution Hall, the conference adjourned without approving the transfer, but participants lost any remaining confidence in the Hoover administration's ability to meet social needs.

Louise was also active in several civic organizations. She served as chair of the Employment and Vocational Guidance Section of the Welfare Council of New York City, an association of non-profit agencies, and joined feminist groups like the American Women's Association and the Women's City Club of New York. The latter hosted an orientation session for women college juniors studying settlement work, unemployment, and social conditions in New York during the summer of 1931, and Louise spoke on the subject of placing disabled workers. The clubhouse at 22 Park Avenue was also the venue for a January 1935 symposium on the effects of the Depression on business and professional women, based on a study by the American Women's Association. Louise and two prominent feminists were on the panel: Ollie Randall, head of the women's division of the Emergency Work and Relief Bureau in New York, and Chase Going Woodhouse, an economist, who was later elected to the U.S. Congress. Such events allowed Louise to stay in touch with the network of professional women that had sustained her throughout her career.[33]

Another member of that network, Frances Perkins, who served as New York State Industrial Commissioner under Governor Franklin Roosevelt, was among those who recognized the need for handicapped employment services and noticed the success of the Center that Louise directed. Convinced that the government ought to take responsibility for and expand the program, Perkins introduced an experiment in public-private cooperation, made possible by the friendship and mutual trust between the two women, who were working together on other employment-related projects. In 1932, the government offered free office space at the public employment office in Brooklyn, allowing the Employment Center for the Handicapped to expand.

Two years later, the Division for the Handicapped of the New York State Employment Service integrated the non-profit Center fully. Louise, whose salary was still paid by private funds, became director of the expanded division and moved into an office in the NYSES Manhattan headquarters at 124 East 28th Street. A report submitted to Franklin Roosevelt's successor as governor, Herbert Lehman in 1935 recognized the success of the division: "Fine employer relationships exist and continuous contact with users of the service is maintained. The large number of placements secured is a real measure of the effectiveness of the working staff and its methods. The service is a credit to those responsible for its operation."[34]

The increase in Louise's responsibilities and public commitments forced her to give up a treasured activity, the Barnard Alumnae Student Loan Committee, which she had chaired from 1927 to 1934. Those were busy years for the committee, which raised money primarily from alumnae, supplemented with occasional grants and loans from other sources, and gave loans in small amounts (less than $200 on average) to advanced students who would not otherwise be able to complete their degree. The Depression increased demand significantly as fathers lost jobs and students found it difficult to earn money through part-time and summer jobs. With other members of the Committee, Louise spent long hours interviewing applicants and agonizing over whom to support and whom to refuse. Having attended Barnard on an academic scholarship, she welcomed the opportunity to help young women complete their education, and she admired the applicants she met, perhaps remembering her own determination and hopes twenty-five years earlier. "Every group that came before us seemed made up of such good material, and at such a fascinating age, both youthful and grownup. ... The variety of things that they want to do!" she told the *Barnard Alumnae Journal*, which interviewed her when she retired from the Committee.[35]

The interviewer for the *Alumnae Journal* was nervous when

she arrived for her meeting with "the leading authority on the placement of the handicapped in this country," but, entering the eight-story red-brick building on 28th Street (which has since become an elegant boutique hotel), she found that "from the elevator man up, everyone is delighted to direct you past rows of outer offices to the inner office of 'L.C.O.'" Obviously, Louise was popular with her staff, and "once in her presence you forget, as she seems to, what a busy woman she is, so unhurried and unstrained is her cordiality, so lively and gracious her manner." In the course of "an interesting and amusing hour," Louise conveyed how much fun she had had "doing pioneer jobs." Her descriptions of her travels and other activities were "full of color, human interest, humor, and above all, a keen social consciousness," and she seemed to enjoy taking the time to tell "her own story of things done and places seen and thoughts thought." The article offers a glimpse of the effect that Louise had on other people and shows that, after decades of hard work and well-earned recognition, she retained her enthusiasm and sense of adventure. She was in fact, once again, about to enter a new field: The interview mentions that she had been "borrowed from the state by the state," and would soon "be devoting a major portion of her time to work on the Governor's Commission on Unemployment Relief."[36]

Chapter XII

Responding to the Depression

New York in Crisis

"34 Social Agencies Seek Aid. Miss Odencrantz Urges Industries to Help in Providing Work" was the headline of an article in the *New York Times* on July 23, 1928. Louise was among those who had noticed that the labor market was deteriorating during the late 1920s—even before the Wall Street crash. As chair of the Employment and Vocational Guidance Section of the Welfare Council of New York, she had helped set up an information office that connected job-seekers with the city's non-profit employment services and attracted "a flood of capable men and women needing work badly." Louise appealed to employment managers of large corporations to utilize the services offered and provide work for people who had been out of work for so long that they were now "literally with their backs to the wall."[1] Public employment bureaus—like the one she had directed a decade earlier—had ceased to function effectively due to underfunding; for the time being, job-seekers had to rely on private agencies despite the high fees they were charging. The information office was a low-cost alternative.

Frances Perkins had also observed that "many people were out of work for longer periods than was comfortable and the turnover was great." As soon as she became Commissioner of Labor, she alerted Governor Roosevelt to the need for "a good modern, well-supported State Public Employment Service, where people would be decently treated and where the business of getting a job could be carried on in an orderly, businesslike, humane way." In June 1929, he agreed to the appointment of an advisory committee to the State Department of Labor, and she invited an "influential body of citizens" to serve, among them Louise. In her letter asking "My Dear Miss Odencrantz," to join the group, Perkins mentioned the "importance of a free public employment service both in periods of industrial depression and in normal times."[2]

At the first meeting of the committee, reported in the *New York Times*, Louise underscored the need for such service, asserting that it could save wage earners the $10,000,000 a year that they were currently paying to 1,200 private agencies in the city.[3] The advisory committee submitted its report in March 1930—after the stock market had crashed and unemployment had increased dramatically—offering a devastating critique of the existing public Bureau of Employment. It "lacks confidence of employers and employees. It pays pitifully low salaries. Its personnel is frequently inert and indifferent … Moreover, it has lacked leadership and any organized supervision and training of its staff. Nor has it evolved any scientific approach to the problem of placement."[4]

While serving on the governor's commission, Louise also addressed groups of concerned citizens. In November 1929, she attended a meeting of the Lower East Side Community Council hosted by the University Settlement on the corner of Eldridge and Rivington Streets, in the same neighborhood as the College Settlement, where she had been a fellow more than twenty years earlier. She knew the other speaker at the event, Richard A. Flinn, who had headed the men's division of the unemployment office in Brooklyn when she was superintendent of the women's section, and who was still on the staff of the New York State Department of Labor. The two disagreed on the situation. Flinn insisted (a month after the stock market crash!) that there was no cause for alarm: "We have the normal amount of unemployment for this time of the year." Louise challenged that assumption and urged action on the recommendation for public works to be initiated in the event of slack employment that the Welfare Council had submitted to Mayor Jimmy Walker more than a year earlier.[5]

The Depression hit New York City particularly hard; by 1932, half of the city's manufacturing plants were closed, one in every three New Yorkers was unemployed, and roughly 1.6 million were on some form of relief.[6] New York, however, was also the first state to take action. In August 1931, the legislature had passed Governor Roosevelt's proposal to create the Temporary Emergency Relief Administration, which provided immediate aid to the unemployed, set up the first public works projects, and established the Home Relief Bureau, administered by local commissioners of public welfare and charged with offering direct assistance such as food, clothing, and medical services. Louise served with twenty-three other social agency executives (including veterans of the settlement movement Mary Simkhovitch and Lillian Wald) on an advisory committee to the Welfare Commissioner. When Mayor Walker of New York closed the city's home relief offices in early January 1932 because they had run out of money, the committee urged that "extraordinary measures be taken if necessary to find the funds needed" to re-open the offices.

"Thousands Face Starvation if Relief is not Restored" was the headline of an article in the *New York Times*, which quoted the statistics provided by the committee and cited its belief that "somewhere in the resources of this great city funds can be found at once to meet the present emergency."[7] Committee members probably knew that the city's debts were so severe that it was borrowing from businesses in order to pay bills, and they might also have known that the mayor himself was under investigation for corruption; he resigned later that year. Despite her support of the committee's appeal to private investors to meet urgent needs, Louise was not impressed with the effect of these efforts; on the back of a photo of Rockefeller Center that she included in a letter to Danish relatives she wrote: "These skyscrapers were built since the Depression started to help the unemployment situation, but it didn't help much." The photo has survived but not the letter, so the message is undated.

Implementing the New Deal

When Franklin Roosevelt became president, the federal government finally began to take action. In June 1933, Congress passed the Wagner-Peyser Act, which established a national system of employment offices, operated by the states under federal supervision and with federal funding. The Act called for an advisory committee charged with "formulating policies and discussing problems relating to employment and insuring impartiality, neutrality and freedom from political influence in the solution of such problems."[8] Robert Maynard Hutchins, president of the University of Chicago, chaired the committee, and Louise was among its fifty members, who gathered in Washington in August for an organizational meeting, addressed by Frances Perkins, Secretary of Labor.

Historians have commented on Roosevelt's and Perkins' shared "predilection for creating committees or boards to get things done."[9] They relied on the expertise and hard work of dedicated citizens to develop and implement government policies. In her work resumé, Louise makes two references to participation in such groups. Under the description of her job with the Center for the Handicapped she mentions that she "served on the U.S. Committee which planned the new Unemployment Insurance Program." A separate note at the end of the resumé ("about 1934-36 served on Advisory Committee for the United States Department of Labor to develop plans for implementing the new Unemployment Insurance and Employment Act passed by Congress"[10]) probably refers to a different committee, related to the implementation of Title III of the 1935 Social Security Act, which authorized the Employment Service to administer unemployment compensation.

Public servants in search of solutions looked to Europe for examples of government responses to social challenges. In September 1934, Louise travelled to Scandinavia and the Soviet Union to investigate employment services in those countries. In an unpublished account, she described the public employment office in Stockholm with great admiration: "Everything looked immaculate and attractive" with good-sized private interviewing rooms, waiting rooms, and offices, and the staff, all civil service, was "of high caliber." Recalling the public relations battle she had fought on behalf of the New York employment service, she noted that "the office has been established so long and is so well known among employers that the manager felt little publicity was necessary."[11]

The glowing praise for the Swedish approach contrasts sharply with a brief paragraph on her subsequent visit to the Soviet Union, which Mary Van Kleeck had probably encouraged her to make. The latter had been greatly impressed with what she saw on a 1932 visit to that country: "There all of the branches of economic life are planned as an integrated whole. It would be worthwhile for us to study its actual technique," she wrote on her return.[12] She saw the Communist economic system as the ultimate implementation of scientific management. Louise had a different impression: "When I reached Moscow, Russia, I enquired for the Public Employment Office, of which a description was given several years ago in *The Survey*. But I was informed that it had been closed because there is no unemployment. A plan has been worked out so that when a factory or other business needs workers, and none are available on its own lists, application is made to other factories, etc."[13] That dismissive "etc." shows how unimpressed she was. Her sense of humor enabled her to see through the pretensions of Soviet central planning. She focused on the needs and potential of individual human beings while Van Kleeck sought theoretical solutions at a macro-level. Despite the disagreement, the two continued to work together professionally.

After her journey, which included her first reunion with relatives in Denmark in 35 years, Louise returned to a busy schedule. Besides serving on federal committees, she continued to support her home state's efforts to cope with the Depression. During the winter of 1934-35, she participated in a study of unemployment relief commissioned by Herbert Lehman, who had succeeded Roosevelt as governor. Among her personal papers, she saved a cartoon by Denys Wortman, famous for his sensitive portrayal of daily life in New York City during the 1930s, which shows a family in a crowded one-room dwelling; the father is holding one baby and coaxing another child to accompany him to the unemployment office: "Come sonny, there'll be lots of other children for you to play with, and as soon as daddy gets a job, we'll all have a house together again."[14] Perhaps she saved the drawing because it reminded her of families she had seen in the intake rooms of the precinct offices, where desperate people were waiting for their cases to be heard and hoping to receive assistance. Its inclusion among her papers emphasizes how she never lost sight of the impact on individuals of the conditions she was observing.

Preparing the report for the governor, Louise and her colleagues applied a methodology similar to the one she had used in her job analysis of social work: observing processes, interviewing staff, studying files and records, accompanying investigators on their rounds, checking the information collected with administrators, case coordinators, office supervisors, and chief clerks to get their views and interpretations, and sharing insights to form a complete picture of precinct functioning and define basic principles. Relief administration should be business-like with regard to economy and efficiency, ensure that only those who were eligible received benefits, and avoid "chiseling" (what present-day critics of government programs call "waste, fraud and abuse"). But it could not "be run on the same basic principles [as] ... private industrial or commercial business" and would have to spend "money without expectation of financial profit." The purpose was to serve the community as well as the client, and the ultimate criterion of success was "conserving human values on which no money valuation can be put."[15]

The basic principles articulated by the Commission in the report submitted to Governor Lehman in June 1935 were those that had guided Louise throughout her career: "respect for individuality and for the basic rights of human beings, a trained understanding of the emotional states of those who seek assistance, [and] an enlightened conception of human needs beyond food and shelter." The report emphasized that "the essence of a proper relief administration ... remains in human relationships—between worker and recipient and between worker and administrative officers."[16]

Louise must have been gratified to work on an urgent contemporary problem with a group of kindred spirits, who shared her understanding that solving problems required a professional and humane approach. They attributed the Temporary Emergency Relief Administration's lack of success to its being "dominated throughout its history by the spirit of improvisation to meet an emergency." Unemployment, they recognized, was *not* a temporary phenomenon, and, even if "so-called normal employment conditions" returned, a "large public relief load" would remain for some years to come. Public relief administration on a vast scale was new in the United States, but it was "imperative that the best possible administrative machinery be planned and erected, the soundest possible policies for granting assistance be introduced and the wisest fiscal procedures be set up."[17] To achieve those goals required training of professionals at every level—a cause that Louise embraced with enthusiasm. She developed qualification guidelines for employment interviewers and taught an extension course at the New York School of Social Work, which had moved into an annex of the Russell Sage Building on 22nd Street.

Shaping a New Profession

Defining strategies, procedures, staff qualifications, training methods, and performance criteria had become Louise's specialty. In 1936, she turned over management of the Center for Handicapped Employment to a successor in order to devote her time to a study of employment offices in the United States for the Social Science Research Council (SSRC). She spent most of the year in Washington D.C., where the SSRC, although headquartered in New York, maintained an office. Her co-authors were Raymond C. Atkinson, who had written an earlier volume on the administration of unemployment compensation published by the SSRC, and Ben Deming, who had been Assistant Director of the Indiana State Employment Service. Recognizing that "the development of an effective unemployment office system is essential to the success of the social security program" the authors set out to "consider the fundamentals of sound organization and administration" necessary to develop such a system and undertook a field survey of nearly 200 public employment offices in twenty-five states.[18] *Public Employment Service in the United States* was published in 1938.

Louise was responsible for the chapters on the training of personnel, on procedures including reception, registration, and placement of applicants, as well as classification and filing of records; she also wrote about services for the inexperienced and the hard-to-place and about inter-state coordination. Her recommendations were practical and concrete, taking into account the perspectives of both clients and staff and aimed at creating a welcoming environment while maintaining efficiency: "It is essential to guard against congestion at the reception point. A low wooden rail may be provided, if necessary, to prevent crowding; but, as a rule, a little ingenuity in planning reception procedures and the arrangement of the reception room will eliminate the necessity for rails."[19]

The interview methods she recommended were those she herself had practiced twenty years earlier in the first Brooklyn employment office and, before then, as a social researcher: "The art of the interviewer lies in his friendly encouragement of the applicant to talk and in his ability to control the interview so that it remains to the point—yielding the necessary information with a minimum of irrelevant conversation." Nevertheless, "a minute or two of commonplace talk at the end of an interview ... often yields a better picture and important new information which the applicant has hesitated to give earlier." Record-keeping and filing systems had come a long way since the "shoe box system" that she had used in the Brooklyn office. By 1935, local offices were using cards supplied by the federal government, designed according to the category of worker (professional, technical, domestic, industrial, agricultural, etc.) and available in different colors for men, women, and veterans. Occupational classifications used for filing must, Louise insisted, be "in sufficient detail to permit convenient and accurate selection of applicants" but "broad enough to cover the usual duties of workers in the given occupation."[20]

Success in matching people and jobs also depended on the collecting and categorizing of information about openings by "experienced interviewers who know what information is essential and how to obtain it by skillful questioning" and who are familiar "with the types of applicants available [and able to discuss them] with the employer." As Louise knew from her own experience, direct contact was essential: Professional field work develops a personal acquaintance between members of the local office staff and employers, creates good will, and stimulates placements. It also enables the employment office personnel to become better acquainted with the characteristics of local industries and occupations.[21]

A reviewer called the book "the most important treatise on public employment service that has appeared in this country since ... 1924. The authors have brought to their task a wealth of experience in administering employment services and a broad knowledge based upon observation of many employment agencies in this country and abroad."[22] Much of the information in the 500-page volume is as antiquated as the technology described (sending Special Delivery letters to applicants that could not be reached by phone, creating number codes to facilitate entering information on punch cards), but the authors' concern for the individuals and communities they serve and their painstaking attention to the details that would allow them to deliver such service effectively are impressive. In the twenty-first century, rhetoric dismissing civil servants as mindless bureaucrats is commonplace. Louise and her colleagues were applying well-tested management practices to the creation of the "administrative state" currently maligned. Their passionate commitment to public service and the essential humanity of their approach inspire admiration.

The next step in Louise's career involved her implementing in practice what she had described in theory. In January 1937, she became Director of Personnel and Training for the New York State Department of Labor, Division of Placement and Unemployment Insurance. She was responsible for selecting and training staff and developing procedures along the lines defined in the SSRC study. It was a job with many challenges. At the beginning of 1937, it looked as if the economy was improving, but by mid-year a downturn set in, and unemployment, which had appeared to be recovering, increased sharply. Employment offices throughout the state were still suffering from many of the shortcomings identified in previous investigations, but the Union of State, County and Municipal Workers pushed back against performance requirements and dismissals. Drawing on her experience in negotiating with unions, Louise helped set up an appeals board, which would consider questions of rating, assignments, and salary and make recommendations to the administration. The union greeted her announcement of the new board in September 1937 as "our first major achievement and a most encouraging precedent."[23]

Meeting the legal demand that heads of local bureaus must pass civil service exams was another challenge. In March 1939, a joint legislative committee in Albany summoned Louise to account for the fact that less than 40 percent of local managers had this qualification. Republicans complained that unqualified staff had been employed on the strength of recommendations from Democratic politicians while Democratic members claimed that the committee was "wasting time" pursuing these enquiries. Caught in the crossfire, Louise kept her cool, explaining that, during the recent decentralization of the unemployment division, qualified senior managers who had been working at the central office in Albany had been assigned to head local offices and were serving temporarily "pending civil service examinations." The hearing concluded with a stern warning that the unemployment division would "get into trouble" if it continued to ignore civil service requirements.[24] The confrontation suggests the political pressures Louise faced as well as the difficulty of finding qualified personnel to provide services for unprecedented numbers of job seekers.

The March 1939 *New York Times* article on the hearing identifies Louise as "superintendent assigned to personnel and training of the Department of Labor, which handles unemployment insurance." Actually, in July 1937, the Division of Placement and Unemployment Insurance had divided personnel administration and training into two bureaus with separate offices. Personnel administration remained in Albany, with a new director, and Louise took charge of the supervision of all training operations, headquartered at 342 Madison Avenue in New York City, which the 1939-1940 *American Women: the Official Who's Who among the Women of the Nation*, lists as her work address. The change in assignment allowed her to focus on the critical task of training, which she talked about in lectures and articles. She urged the New York School of Social Work to set up extension courses throughout the state for persons currently serving as interviewers at employment offices and those applying for such jobs. In a speech to the Welfare Council of New York City, she insisted that training should focus on practice: "The important thing [is] to break through routines and procedures, to a basic understanding of relationships, reasons and values."[25]

Lecturing on "Recent Developments in Employment Services" to a December 1939 Metropolitan Conference, she emphasized the need for "training of personnel in the performance of insurance and placement functions ... due to the fact that comparatively few persons were available who had experience in these fields, and the additional new personnel had to be drawn from other fields and trained within the new organization." The conclusion of that paper, reprinted in *Occupations, the Vocational Guidance Magazine*, January 1940, reflects her excitement about the challenge she faced: "Many problems have yet to be solved. ... Perhaps the most fascinating feature of this work is the fact that it is a growing thing which requires the thinking and contribution of the personnel engaged in it, as well as those who are otherwise interested in it."[26]

Chapter XIII

Finding a Place to Call Home

Transitions

By the late 1930s, Marguerite was the only Odencrantz sibling with a permanent residence in New York City. She and her husband had bought a townhouse in Brooklyn, where her parents moved in after selling their farm in New Jersey, and where Louise also lived for a while (it is listed as her home address in the 1939 *Who's Who* entry). Tulla was working as statistician for the New York State Department of Health and living at an apartment in Albany, which provided a convenient place for her sister to stay when she had meetings in the capital. Fred lived in Camden, New Jersey, with his wife and son.

In May 1939, all of the siblings gathered at the bedside of their mother, who was dying at the age of 85. According to Marguerite's description of the scene, even in her final moments, Frederikke appeared to stay in control of events as she had throughout her long life: "[Mother] was always dramatic in relating her adventures and was so to the end. A few moments before she expired, a noise came from her throat. She looked at her grieving family surrounding her bed and announced, '*That* was the death rattle!' and so it was."[1] Gustaf, who had depended on his strong-willed wife's support throughout their marriage, lived another three years and was apparently in good health until his death at the age of 94—despite the malaria that he had contracted in Texas during the 1890s. While they were still living at the Raven Rock farm, he and Frederikke had selected a gravesite at nearby Rosemont Cemetery, where local residents had been buried since the early eighteenth century. The quiet, rural setting, surrounded by farmland, might have reminded her of the graveyard at her father's village church in Denmark. Neither she nor Gustaf had returned to Scandinavia since the 1899 visit. They had chosen America, and their children had become Americans without any sense of dual identity.

Shortly after her mother's death, Louise moved into the Parkside, a residential hotel for women at 18 Gramercy Park South. The location, around the corner from the Russell Sage Foundation on 22nd Street, where she often attended meetings, allowed her to stay in touch with her professional network. Through those connections, she found a position as executive director for the Social Work Vocational Bureau, a newly established non-profit organization providing counselling and placement for social workers, funded in part by the Russell Sage Foundation. There is no record of her reason for leaving the Department of Labor job, but perhaps she felt that she had achieved what she wanted—creating a functioning division—and just managing it was less exciting, or perhaps she was tired of shuttling back and forth between Albany and New York and eager to settle down and stay in one place. She enjoyed living in Gramercy Park, but the room at the Parkside was only a temporary residence. Would it be possible to find an apartment in the neighborhood?

On the corner of 22nd Street and Second Avenue, a large seventeen-story apartment building had opened in 1931. It had a colorful Art Deco façade, a spacious entrance hall with a reception desk and a doorman on duty, a roof terrace with a splendid view of the Manhattan skyline, and bright, modern apartments with shiny hardwood floors and fireplaces. The idea of a comfortable, permanent home in a neighborhood associated with much of her career appealed to Louise. She had worked at the Russell Sage Foundation building (now known as Sage House) on the corner of Lexington Avenue when it first opened in 1912, done research in the library for her study of social work during the 1920s, and, later, when she held other positions, returned for meetings there. The United Charities Building at the corner of 22nd and Park Avenue South had been a magnet for other Progressive Era organizations. The Manhattan Trade School for Girls, where she had collected data for her M.A. thesis, had moved from its earlier site on 23rd Street into a purpose-built structure at #123 in 1915; the same year, the first Children's Court of New York opened at #137. Finding an apartment on East 22nd Street would satisfy her dual longing, expressed in the quote from Alvin Johnson's biography that she copied and saved: a yearning for a place to call home and "an equally deep and powerful desire for what lies beyond the horizon." She would be able to put down roots in a neighborhood associated with the causes that had taken her beyond the horizon.

Paying the rent on a one-bedroom apartment alone would be a stretch, however. Tulla's job with the state government would keep her in Albany, so, for the first time in her life, Louise looked for a roommate outside her family. Her friend Ruth Reticker, who worked for the Social Security Administration in Washington D.C., was sharing a house with a fellow University of Chicago graduate, Lois Olson. Ruth introduced Louise to the latter's sister Helen, who had taken a job in New York and was looking for a place to stay. Helen moved into the apartment Louise had rented, and the two lived together for the next 27 years—an arrangement similar to that of many professional women of their generation. In *Testament of Friendship*, British writer Vera Brittain, who roomed with the novelist Winifred Holtby after they graduated from Oxford in 1921, describes the pleasure of "coming home at the end of the day after a series of separate varied experiences, and each recounting these incidents to the other over late biscuits and tea."[2]

Louise, Ruth and the Olson sisters were more likely to do their sharing over cocktails, but the companionship was equally important, and so was the independence that they built into their accommodations. Ruth had an architect design her house in Chevy Chase, D.C. to provide common areas and a bedroom/study for herself on the first floor and a large room with its own fireplace upstairs for Lois. Defining separate space in a small New York apartment was more challenging, but possible: Helen had the master bedroom, where she kept her desk, books, and pictures, and Louise, whose heirlooms furnished the living room, slept in the small dining room next to the kitchen. She had moved frequently, but she would stay at 235 East 22nd Street for the rest of her life.

The new job seemed to be a good fit for Louise. Connecting people with jobs and creating conditions that enabled them to function effectively had been the central focus of her career since 1915. She had brought the perspective of social work to those activities and published a job analysis of casework. Heading an organization dedicated to the professional development and placement of social workers would allow her to integrate and draw upon her previous experience, and—as always—she welcomed the opportunity to meet new challenges. The field had changed, however, since she published her book in 1928. New Deal programs expanded services such as public assistance, child welfare, aid to the aged, care for handicapped children, and social work in the schools. As the economy improved, basic social needs became less urgent, but social agencies had added counseling and casework on a fee-paid basis to their activities, and the public had come to expect these services. As a result, there was a shortage of qualified professionals. The situation facing Louise in her new position was the opposite of the one she had confronted previously as administrator of employment agencies: Then she had to persuade employers to hire the applicants that came to her; now the problem was finding qualified candidates to fill positions.

U.S. entry into World War II brought new demands for social programs to serve men and women in the armed forces and their families. The Social Work Vocational Bureau received thousands of requests for competent professionals in public and private agencies, but enrollment in training programs for social workers declined as work opportunities in other fields increased, and college graduates preferred well-paid jobs to further education. Salaries for social workers lagged behind those for other professionals with advanced degrees although they had increased from a median of $1,800 in 1941 to $2,400 in 1944. That, however, was still a modest figure—comparable to $35,445 in 2020 when the median annual wage for social workers was $51,760. The situation was dire, Louise wrote in a September 1945 article: "Hundreds of local agencies as well as national and international programs are seriously handicapped in urgently needed services because of lack of qualified workers."[3]

The conclusion of the war would increase demands because returning veterans would need medical and psychiatric social workers, and thousands of trained leaders would be needed "for the vast program of relief and rehabilitation in war devastated countries."

As head of a national agency, Louise saw little hope for improvement in the immediate future and predicted that "with the demobilization of the armed forces and war industries, and the resulting social and economic problems, the personnel shortage in social work is likely to become worse rather than better." Her only hope was a call for "cooperative efforts to develop a more adequate supply, for in the last analysis the effectiveness of any social service program rests upon the skills and knowledge of those who administer it."[4]

As always, Louise emphasized the contributions and perspective of individual employees. Unfortunately for the success of her agency, when those individuals did not find their skills and knowledge to be valued, they looked for other jobs. In fact, the shortage of social workers was due not only to the lack of people entering the field but to high turnover among professionals who were frustrated with "routinized paperwork, heavy caseloads, low wages, and limited mobility" according to historian Daniel Walkowitz. He entitles his chapter on the war years "The Evisceration of the Professional Worker Identity."[5]

Besides these issues, the Bureau struggled with declining support from foundations. An article in *The Compass* (a professional journal for social work) commended the organization for increasing membership and trying "valiantly to serve the casework field against great odds" although it "had to operate on a very restricted annual budget."[6] Financial issues led the governing board to re-examine the Bureau's functions and focus on maintaining personnel records while eliminating counseling and referral services. That decision, effective January 1947, may have precipitated Louise's resignation in November 1946. The president of the board, Helen Crosby, was a fellow Barnard graduate, who had served with Louise on alumnae committees, but there may have been tensions between the two. Crosby's announcement, cited in a professional journal under the heading, "Social Work Vocational Bureau Curtails Services" makes no reference to the work accomplished during Louise's tenure.[7]

Shrinking resources and the narrowing of objectives meant that the job was not fun anymore; it was not the kind of challenge that Louise had welcomed throughout her career, one that she could meet through the application of vigor, common sense, and creativity. Although she had never worked long enough at any one job to collect a pension, she had saved and inherited money and invested it well, so she would be able to live modestly but comfortably without earning a salary. *The Survey Midmonthly* reported her retirement in a prominent entry, accompanied by a photo (unlike other personnel change announcements on the same page), mentioning that "Miss Odencrantz has been an outstanding figure in the field of employment and personnel since 1915."[8] She cared passionately about many other issues and causes, and at the age of sixty-two she had a lot of energy to invest in them.

Active Retirement

Organizations with an international focus, committed to creating a new world order and providing relief and assistance to countries and individuals suffering the consequences of war, had always held special appeal for Louise. The first item on the list of post-retirement volunteer activities in her work resumé is service on the national board of the YWCA. A member of the association since her undergraduate days, she shared its concern with youth employment, vocational training, literacy, and the problems of women industrial workers as well as its overall goal, articulated by one of its leaders: "to help people equip themselves with the knowledge, skill and spirit necessary for responsible action towards shaping their own lives and the future of their communities and nations."[9] That statement emphasizes the association's international outreach. Immediately after the end of World War II, the YWCA initiated refugee services and other emergency measures to help reconstruction, and, later, it cooperated with United Nations agencies in order to extend those services to developing countries.

Serving on the YWCA national board also engaged Louise in the emerging campaign against racism. In 1946, the association had adopted an "Interracial Charter" establishing that "wherever there is injustice on the basis of race, whether in the community, the nation, or the world, our protest must be clear and our labor for its removal, vigorous and steady." Three years later, the National Convention pledged that "the YWCA will work for integration and full participation of minority groups in all phases of American life."[10] There is no record of Louise's specific involvement with these issues, but she was a firm supporter of the civil rights movement throughout the 1950s and 1960s.

Louise was active in other international organizations, including the Women's International League for Peace and Freedom (WILPF), founded by Jane Addams after World War I, and the United World Federalists, which advocated peace through disarmament and promoted a system of federal world government through the United Nations. She knew that these goals were utopian and elusive. "The United World Federalists are concentrating on the elimination of nuclear tests as is also the WILPF," she wrote in 1959. "It is slow, discouraging work. We plan meetings, but so few people seem to be concerned about the future, or they feel that what they can do doesn't count. But we keep plugging away, and perhaps the next generation may see something accomplished." References to these organizations in subsequent letters to her Danish relative, who was also a member of the WILPF, reflect the same hope that common sense, which she had applied to social and economic problems during her working life, would also be the solution to international issues if only people of good will worked hard enough at it. "We are all active with the United World Federalists and trying to get our country to make more effort towards disarmament and stopping nuclear tests. It all seems so senseless, but how to stop it is the question," she wrote later that year.[11]

International cooperation to provide welfare services was an important component of post-war recovery. Understanding the needs of people throughout the world and planning how to meet them were the subjects of a December 1952 world conference of social workers in Madras (now Chennai), India. Eleanor Roosevelt devoted her column "My Day" on October 11 to the upcoming event, stressing the practical and realistic approach of the organizers as well as their recognition "that no world can survive if people are deprived of their rights to human dignity, opportunity and security."[12] Louise participated in the conference, joining a delegation of alumni from the Columbia School of Social Work. She had always seen social work as a means of improving the quality of life for the community as well as the individual, and the conference emphasis on the role of social service in raising the standards of living appealed to her.

Louise was excited about her first visit to Asia. In a letter to her Danish cousin Marianne, she wrote that she was postponing the trip to Europe that she had been planning for some time. Instead, she was "leaving New York by boat to London on Nov. 15, and then flying to India. I am coming back by boat over the Pacific so that I can see a bit of Singapore, Hong Kong and Japan. I will be away until February 15, and at Christmas I will be in Ceylon. I have never been to the Far East, so this will be all new to me."[13] (The letter is dated five days after the death of Marianne's son. The fact that Louise wrote as soon as she heard about the loss from Marianne's brother Soren, who was living in New York, indicates how close she felt to the Danish relatives although she had not seen them since 1934; the Asian journey was obviously a big event in her life since she mentioned it in a letter of condolence.)

Although it had been more than twenty years since Louise attended an international conference, she must have felt at home immediately among colleagues from all over the world and enjoyed the busy schedule of plenary sessions, discussion groups, and cultural events. She would have found two keynote speakers especially congenial. Chester Bowles, who had served in several U.N. posts before becoming U.S. ambassador to India, emphasized that "for better or for worse, we are living in one world" and expressed the hope that the change that would occur within the next ten years in what were still referred to as "underdeveloped" areas would "be a revolution of non-violence, evolution and understanding" rather than one of "violence and destruction." Alva Myrdahl, who had been active in developing social welfare policies in Sweden during the 1930s and was head of UNESCO's social science section, spoke about education as a pre-requisite for the improvement of living standards and about the need for coordination of educational and social reforms, economic investments, and efforts to improve health.[14]

The conference recommended approaches familiar to Louise and her contemporaries from their efforts to improve the lives of American workers since the early years of the century. One session advocated the participation of university students in voluntary social services—like the settlement workers in New York and other U.S. cities. Another concluded that the skills and techniques of social workers could help raise standards of living in the underdeveloped world, but only if the experts listened to local people's own insights—just as Louise had in interviews with immigrant women workers. Arguments about improving industrial relations, adapting welfare services to industry, and recognizing the correlation between better working conditions and productivity must have reminded her of her experience as personnel manager during the 1920s, and she probably contributed to the discussion about rehabilitation of the physically handicapped, which pleaded for a change in the public attitude towards disabled workers and for their training and vocational guidance.

The *Indian Journal of Social Work* published a detailed report on the six-day conference. Reading this account in the twenty-first century, after decades of more or less successful efforts to further economic and social development, one is struck by the optimism with which the delegates addressed the issues. At the opening, the chair of the reception committee said, "Social work is an ideal platform for international co-operation, for the human heart is quick to respond to suffering. It is for social work to relieve and alleviate suffering and herald the creation of a world order when people can live in peace and happiness." At the closing plenary, before everybody joined in singing "Auld Lang Syne," the chair of the conference declared "What we have to do in this world is to restore the faith in man ... through the field of social work, we can help to do it more effectively than through any other kind of service."[15] Louise would have agreed with that statement. Faith in the ability of human beings to meet challenges and contribute to their community if they were given the chance had been the foundation of all her work.

The conference organizers were proud to host the first international gathering of social workers held in Asia and pleased that guests would be able "to take from India as much as they could give her in the realm of culture, education, literature, art and social life."[16] The program included events that introduced participants to Indian culture such as a performance by Rukmani Devi Arundale, a well-known artist, credited with the revival of Indian classical dance. Indian life and culture would remain a major interest of Louise's. Back in New York, she joined the board of the Whiting India Guilds, an organization that imported handicrafts made by Indian women such as silk scarves, cotton fabrics, jewelry, and ornaments of exotic woods to be sold through charitable institutions. In 1953, the president of Barnard invited "Miss Louise Odencrantz, who has travelled extensively in India," to attend a luncheon for Lady D. Rama Rau, who was receiving an award from Columbia University for her promotion of women's rights in her home country.[17]

Louise had continued to be involved in Barnard activities despite her many other commitments. Retirement freed her to assume a more active role. She chaired the Alumnae Vocational Guidance Committee, "composed of eight to ten alumnae experienced in vocational guidance and personnel work," which acted "as an advisory group to the Placement Office and the Student Vocational Committee."[18] The committee was conscious of the needs of women who had married immediately after graduation, had never held a job and wanted to find work later in life — a subject Louise covered in a *Barnard Alumnae Monthly* article entitled "Over 35? Housewife? No Experience?"[19]

In a later article, she recommended social work as an appropriate field for "mature women," promising that "the work is always varied and interesting." (The article is accompanied by a photo of a stern-looking Louise with the caption: "An expert offers a solid lead.")[20] At her fiftieth reunion that year, she spoke about all that she had forgotten of what she once learned in differential calculus and advanced economics courses but insisted she could still "recall every name on the roll call of both of those classes."[21] Barnard had given her knowledge, but she had also learned not to take intellectual accomplishments too seriously. The fact that she remembered the names of the girls in her class indicates the centrality of individual human beings in her life and her work.

Chapter XIV

Connecting with Danish Relatives and Coping with Old Age

A Personal Perspective

In 1956, Louise was able to make the journey to Scandinavia that she had postponed because of the Madras conference. Her Washington friend Ruth Reticker joined her on the trip. Together, they took a cruise of the Norwegian fjords, toured new urban developments, social institutions, and employment services in Sweden and Denmark to satisfy the professional interests they shared, met colleagues they had last seen at conferences of the International Industrial Relations Association during the 1920s, and explored Copenhagen and its environs. Louise was excited to connect with Danish relatives she had not seen since 1934 and with those who were born after that time, myself among them. I was fourteen years old, and her visit gave me my first chance to use the English I had learned at school; she listened patiently to my efforts, and we got along very well. After the reunion, she began writing regularly to my mother Bodil, her cousin's daughter, who shared many of her interests.

A few years later, when I received a grant for a year of study at Connecticut College, Louise invited me to stay with her in New York before the start of the semester. I got to know her well during the two weeks that I spent at her apartment in September 1960 and during subsequent visits to what became my home away from home. Writing this biography, I have often wished that I had asked more questions about her life, but I was only eighteen at the time and had been raised to think that it was not polite for young people to ask too many questions. I experienced her as a vibrant, charming, elderly woman, keenly interested in events and people, ready to listen, but with strong opinions, surrounded by friends, and, without seeming domineering or controlling, able to organize things effectively—characteristics and behaviors that I have noticed in my study of her career.

Louise met me at the pier the morning I arrived in New York on the same Norwegian American liner that had brought her to Denmark four years earlier. She had organized everything for my arrival but was disappointed that we had to wait a long time for the customs officer to inspect my luggage. "I'm sorry you had such a bad reception from our government," she said. That statement, I now realize, reflected a fundamental attitude of hers: The U.S. Customs Service was a branch of *her* government, and, if it did not perform well, she was responsible. Everything else went smoothly. Mary, the wife of her cousin Soren, who had been waiting outside the arrival building with her car, drove us to 235 East 22nd Street, where the doorman arranged for some of my suitcases to be stored. Helen, who shared the apartment, had vacated her room so that I could stay there while she slept on the couch in the living room. I realized that people liked doing things for Louise. After dinner, the three of us went up to the roof terrace of the building, which had a splendid view of Midtown Manhattan. Louise pointed out the famous buildings around us, as excited about introducing me to the city she loved as I was to see these sights for the first time.

Eager that I should have a good impression of New York, Louise sent me off to explore the city with instructions about subways and bus lines, written on the back of scraps of paper cut from the reports of organizations of which she was a member. She trusted my ability to get around the metropolis on my own (as she had done when she arrived there as a teenager) and was exercising the management skills she had practiced throughout her career: Make sure people know what they are doing and leave them to get on with it. While giving me independence, she also took me to cultural events that she herself enjoyed. We saw the French mime artist Marcel Marceau perform, and she laughed heartily as the character "Bip," Marceau's alter ego, wearing his trademark top hat with a red flower, struggled with the invisible obstacles on the stage that he shaped for us through his movements. We also attended a production of *The Miracle Worker*, in which Anne Bancroft portrayed Annie Sullivan's struggle to teach the blind and deaf Helen Keller to communicate—a subject of special interest to Louise because of her work with the Employment Center for the Handicapped.

September 1960 was an exciting time in American politics, and Louise followed events with keen interest. She read the *New York Times* thoroughly, listened to radio broadcasts throughout the day, and watched the CBS evening news. Her running commentary made it quite clear what she thought of angry demonstrators against school integration in New Orleans and of Soviet Premier Khrushchev haranguing the UN General Assembly (the famous speech during which he banged his shoe on the podium). A lifelong Democrat, she would have preferred Adlai Stevenson at the top of the Democratic ticket, but she supported Kennedy after he was nominated and took me to a rally for him at the Waldorf Astoria. Her concern was not only with major political events but with local issues, large and small. She complained that women released from prison were only given fifteen cents for a bus ride— "not even enough for a transfer!" —and told me that "New York City has a lot of dirty politics, so all of us have to work to clean it up." The statement reflected her sense of responsibility; it was not enough to complain about things, you had to do something about them, and she enjoyed being part of the process: "Always some cause to work for, but anyway it makes life exciting," she said.

Louise enjoyed introducing me to her friends, many of whom lived in her building and often gathered at her apartment for cocktails and snacks. In a letter to my mother she expressed the hope that I did not mind having "to endure so many old ladies, all of whom liked to see some one of the younger generation. We have all too little contact."[1] She had no need to apologize—the friends were a diverse group with interesting backgrounds. Some knew Louise through professional associations, including Edith Dudley, a former colleague from the New York State Employment Service, and Elmina Lucke, who had founded and directed the Delhi School of Social Work, lived in India for several years, and known Mahatma Gandhi personally (she had been with him the evening before his assassination). Some were younger than Louise, e.g. Louise Brewer, whose profile in her 1997 obituary was typical of the group: "lifelong commitment to politics and activism ... worked for numerous Democratic Party candidates on local and national campaigns ...

worked in the Peace Movement and was deeply concerned with issues of the elderly."[2] These women were kindred spirits, and it was obvious that they had deep respect and affection for Louise.

Louise's network of friends extended beyond New York City, and she arranged for me to stay with several of them during the summer after college when I took a bus trip across the United States. My itinerary was ambitious; "don't make fun of Americans visiting a dozen countries in a month; you're covering a continent in four weeks!" she teased me, but she was eager to hear about my adventures when I got back to New York to spend a few days before going home to Denmark. Saying good-bye was sad for both of us. We could not have anticipated that I would return five years later with my American husband and settle in Washington, D.C. She encouraged us to visit "235" whenever we could. As always, she organized everything efficiently, found a vacant apartment for us to stay in and a garage for our car, and engaged in lively conversations about what was happening in the world and about our plans for graduate school and teaching jobs.

Old Age Catches Up

"Chairs, chairs everywhere, and not a place to sit," Louise complained after visiting an exhibition of Scandinavian furniture, echoing Coleridge's Ancient Mariner ("Water, water everywhere nor any drop to drink"). Her legs were bothering her, and she found it difficult to stand or walk for long periods. In a January 1962 letter, she admitted that she was "beginning to show her years," but looked forward to attending an evening performance at the Metropolitan Opera with Helen despite the fact that it required a good deal of walking. (It would never occur to her to take a cab: "subways are part of our way of life," she used to say.) During the 1963-64 season, she attended several concerts including one with Arthur Rubenstein, "who at 75 is as energetic as ever"—more than she could say for herself. It was her first visit to the newly opened Lincoln Center; she found the stairs difficult, and, in her usual activist spirit, telephoned the management to complain that the steps, used by many older people, had no railings. Reluctantly, however, she recognized that old age not only limited her mobility but her direct involvement in causes that she cared about: "I am afraid I am a backslider as I now don't do anything in any organizations except pay a few dues. I guess it is age galloping upon me. But I guess the world can't expect much of us oldsters up in the 80s."[3]

Throughout her life, Louise had been close to her sisters, who were living in separate apartments in Queens. Marguerite, who had been a widow for many years, was enjoying an active retirement, but Tulla became increasingly reclusive. Finally, the sisters found a nursing home for her. Louise continued to visit her regularly, but Marguerite moved to California to join her son and his young family there. Their brother Fred had been living in Florida for years and never visited New York, so, by 1967, the only relatives remaining in the city besides Tulla were Louise's cousin Soren and his wife Mary. Soren was old and frail and nearly blind, but he and Louise were fond of each other and enjoyed lively arguments about issues on which they disagreed.

Increasingly, Louise depended on Helen, who had retired but stayed engaged with the political and other organizations that she and Louise supported, allowing the latter to be involved vicariously. On January 5, 1968, Helen had lunch at home before leaving for an appointment at a neighborhood beauty parlor. An hour later, the hairdresser phoned and asked Louise to come by because "something had happened." Fearing what it might be, she asked her friend and neighbor Edith Dudley to go with her, and, when they got to the shop, they learned that Helen had passed away. Louise was devastated. She and Helen had shared an apartment for 27 years, and she had hoped that the latter would look after her in her declining years. Helen's sister Lois came up from Washington, and friends gathered for a memorial service at the Unitarian Community Church of New York. Later that spring, Louise received another shock: her cousin Soren died. She attended his memorial service at the same church and was moved by the pastor's eulogy. "Dr. Harrington is always so sympathetic," she told her Danish relative.[4]

Meanwhile, friends and neighbors at "235" rallied to Louise's support. Edith Dudley took her out for a short walk every day, and others stopped by to see her in the afternoon. She began looking at nursing homes and visited one where many of her friends were living but was relieved when there was no immediate vacancy. By

April, she was feeling well enough to spend Easter with a friend in the country. Her brother Fred's son Kirk, a nuclear physicist living in California, with whom she had not had much contact since he was a boy, came for a visit. She hoped that, when she went to the retirement home, he would want some of her furniture, including pieces from her father's childhood home in Sweden. Putting her affairs in order was on her mind, and she assembled two sets of records of her career, one for the Schlesinger Library at Harvard and one for Esther Peterson, head of the United States Women's Bureau at the Department of Labor.

Although Louise complained that she did not have much energy and that her legs were stiff and slow, she tried to be positive ("my old limbs hang together") and enjoyed sitting in the roof garden of her building or going for short walks with Edith. Most of the time, she wrote, "I stay home and look at TV, and my friends come to visit, and there is so much to read. And a few friends like to play bridge." She continued to follow political events, regretting that she could not take a more active role: "We have our political problems, all of which seem so uncertain—almost without solution. We don't seem to have enough brains, and no one seems to have any practical possible solutions. But I don't propose to solve them!" Although she opposed the Vietnam War, she found some of the student protests "pointless" and worried that they interfered "with the many students who want to study. Our Columbia University has been badly hit and disorganized." (More than sixty years after she had received her M.A. there, Columbia was still *our* university!) She did not, however, give up hope that common sense would eventually prevail and continued to support the United World Federalists, which she included in her will. The 1968 presidential election engaged her, and she was deeply disappointed with the outcome. "I worked very hard to get HHH into the presidency and am very pessimistic, as are many people, about Nixon. But somehow we survive these crises!" she wrote after the election.[5]

Louise put the nursing home decision on hold at the beginning of 1969 when a friend introduced her to a young Yugoslav woman, who had recently immigrated to the United States and was looking for a job. She moved into Helen's room and did the shopping and cooking for Louise, who appreciated the assistance and the companionship: "She has been wonderful to me and so thoughtful," she wrote to Marguerite in March, adding "I don't see many people—except those here in the house. My own friends—from college—are all too lame, sick or in nursing homes. And the younger ones have jobs. But there is always the telephone." As always, she tried to strike a positive note, mentioning that Edith had taken her for a walk around the block that day for the first time after a long period of cold weather. Her legs were very stiff, "but I *hope* they'll improve."[6]

Shortly after writing this letter, Louise was hospitalized, and, on April 7, she died "of bone decalcification complicated by pulmonary edema" according to her obituary in the *New York Times*.[7]

Epilogue

Louise had specifically asked that there be no funeral ceremony, but her friends organized a memorial service at the Unitarian Community Church of New York, where Helen's service had also been held. Tulla could not leave her nursing home, and neither Marguerite nor Fred was able to travel. So the only occupants of the pew reserved for "family" were Mary, her cousin Soren's widow, and me. But the church was full of people who had come to celebrate her life. I recognized her friends from the apartment building, but I did not know the others, and there was no social event afterwards where I might have learned who they were. She had left instructions that her ashes should be scattered (I am not sure where).

The minister of the Community Church, Donald Harrington, gave the eulogy at the memorial service. He was an active supporter of many of the same social and political causes as Louise, and it is clear from his characterization of her that they knew each other: "She was interested in everything, inside and outside of her field, and thus was an endlessly interesting person. She was fully alive, and very lively, and one of the most delightful conversationalists I have ever known. ... She loved people and devoted her life to her work, her friends, and her fellowmen." Yet there is a note of condescension in his praise: "She was a sweet, quiet and very dear, womanly woman. She moved among us quietly, and she did her great work in the world unobtrusively, but with a most remarkable inner strength and character. She was one of the great feminists of our time, and yet somehow she did not fit the image of the feminist, for she was shy and sweet and there was nothing overbearing about her."[1]

Harrington may have resented the assertive feminists of the 1960s and wanted to show that Louise was different, and it is possible that, in their conversations, she adapted to his expectations—a sign of her ability to get along with people. She had not, however, been "shy and sweet" when she inspected factories, pointed out dangerous practices, walked into tenement homes and sat down to dinner with immigrant families, negotiated agreements with striking weavers, promoted employment for women and disabled workers in interviews and speeches, voiced her disagreement with officials who downplayed the impact of the Depression, and responded to criticism in the New York State Assembly. Even Harrington's acknowledgment of her pathbreaking work is somewhat dismissive: "She was a pioneer in many respects in what we now call social work," suggesting that social work was not quite recognized as a profession and ignoring the other fields in which Louise was also a pioneer. He seems to relegate her to the obscurity that has swallowed the achievement of many women.

Despite their patronizing tone, however, some of Harrington's comments contain an element of truth. His statement that Louise did her work "unobtrusively" is not quite accurate but underscores the point that, while she was a frequent and effective public speaker and used the media to increase awareness and understanding of the issues she cared about, her goal was to call attention to the work, to the people she was trying to serve, not to herself and her achievement. What mattered to her was helping people and making the world a better place, not to get credit for her efforts. Her feminism was less about gaining rights for women and more about allowing them and other marginalized groups to develop and use their talents for their own benefit and in the service of their community. Her vision was not utopian but pragmatic: Do not wait for the perfect plan, but get started; gather the facts, listen to all stakeholders, identify shared interests, and build structures that enable people to meet challenges and cope with emergencies. She knew reality would always be messy, but she trusted that if we applied common sense and talked with each other, we could find solutions that allowed all members of society to contribute and benefit.

What George Eliot said of her heroine Dorothea at the end of *Middlemarch* might be said of Louise: "The effect of her being on those around her was incalculably diffusive: for the growing good of the world is partly dependent on unhistoric acts; and that things are not so ill with you and me as they might have been, is half owing to the number who lived faithfully a hidden life, and rest in unvisited tombs." Louise and her contemporaries—with the exception of Frances Perkins—are not familiar figures, but their achievements have benefitted subsequent generations. They opened new career paths for women, developed procedures and standards for those fields, and earned professional respect. They supported data-based reforms and the creation of an effective public safety net, and they helped reduce industry hazards and increase attention to employee welfare, thus transforming the American workplace. Libertarian arguments against "regulations" have dominated the political discourse during recent decades, but new voices are expressing ideas remarkably similar to those heard a century ago. The cohort of women economists joining the Democratic administration in 2021 share their predecessors' combination of intellectual rigor, professional competence and experience, and commitment to the common good.

Notes

Introduction

1. *1907 Class Book. 1907–1912*, Barnard Digital Collection, accessed through http://www.irwincollier.com/barnard-b-columbia-m-labor-economist-louise-c-odencrantz-1907-1912.
2. Miller, Alice Duer, *Barnard College/the First Fifty Years* (New York: Columbia University Press, 1939), 36.
3. Ruth Richards, "Projections: Louise C. Odencrantz," *Barnard College Alumnae Monthly*, XXIV (February 1935), 8.

Chapter I

1. Alvin Johnson, *Pioneer's Progress* (New York: Viking Press, 1952), chapter 23.
2. Quotes in this chapter are from Frederikke Odencrantz, unpublished memoir, transcribed by Marguerite Stockbauer, in family archive.

Chapter II

1. Unless otherwise indicated, quotes in this chapter are from Marguerite Stockbauer's notes to her transcription of her mother's memoir.
2. Fred Odencrantz inherited the portrait of his grandmother; his son gave it to the Gothenburg Museum. Louise inherited the portrait of Pastor Smith, which is now in the author's possession.
3. Frederikke Odencrantz, unpublished memoir.
4. Letter from Jeanette Odencrantz, Louise Odencrantz' private papers, in family archive.
5. *Sunday Tribune*, April 2, 1916, MC 195, folder 16, Louise C. Odencrantz Papers, 1909-1968, Schlesinger Library, Radcliffe Institute, Harvard University, Cambridge, Mass. https://id.lib.harvard.edu/ead/sch00834/catalog.
6. Gary Hermalyn, *Morris High School and the Creation of the New York City*

Public High School System (New York: The Bronx County Historical Society, 1995), 113-16.
7   Ibid., 76.
8   Marguerite's epilogue to transcription of Frederikke's memoir.
9   Quoted in Duer Miller, 172.
10 Description of entrance exam in *Barnard College Catalog, 1903*.

Chapter III

1   Marian Churchill White, *History of Barnard* (New York: Columbia University Press, 1954), 35
2   *Barnard Bulletin*, October 1903.
3   White, 29.
4   Rosalind Rosenberg, *Changing the Subject, How the Women of Columbia Shaped the Way We Think about Sex and Politics* (New York: Columbia University Press, 2004), 58. The first African-American student at Barnard was Zora Neale Hurston, who graduated in 1928 at the age of 37.
5   Duer Miller, 46, 36
6   Ibid., 68.
7   Iid., 41.
8   Ibid., 39.
9   Richards, "Projections," 8.
10 Duer Miller, 158.
11 Course descriptions from Barnard catalog
12 John Bates Clark, *The Distribution of Wealth: A Theory of Wages, Interest and Profits* (New York: The Macmillan Company, 1899), 281-82. 281-82.
13 The quotes are from Henry Rogers Seager, *Social Insurance: A Program of Social Reform* (New York: Macmillan, 1910), 84, 89; the book was based on his lectures.
14 Duer Miller, 158.
15 Josephine Goldmark, *Impatient Crusader: Florence Kelley's Life Story* (Urbana: University of Illinois Press, 1953), 72.
16 The *Barnard Bulletin*, 12/12/1906, reported on the tea in the theater, but there is no transcript of Kelley's presentation at Barnard. The quotes are from a speech she gave in Philadelphia on July 22, 1905, available at https://awpc.cattcenter.iastate.edu/2017/03/09/child-labor-womens-suffrage-july-22-1905, accessed May 1, 2020.
17 Ibid.
18 National Consumers League website, accessed 9/22/2021, www.nclnet.org/history.
19 *Barnard Bulletin*, 12/12/1906.
20 Ibid., quoting College Settlement Association officer Elsa Herzfeld.

21 Marguerite Stockbauer's introduction to Frederikke's unpublished memoir.
22 *Barnard Bulletin,* 5/15/1907; *New York Times,* 5/9/1907.
23 George Eliot, *Mill on the Floss* (1860), chapter V.

Chapter IV

1 Robert A. Woods and Albert J. Kennedy, editors, *Handbook of Settlements* (New York: Russell Sage Foundation, 1911), 193.
2 Allen F. Davis, *Spearheads for Reform, The Social Settlements and the Progressive Movement, 1890-1914* (New Brunswick: Rutgers University Press, 1984), 31-32, 244-45.
3 *Columbia University Bulletin,* 1907.
4 The figures are from Louise Odencrantz, "The Irregularity of Employment of Women Factory Workers," *The Survey,* (May 1909): 196-210.
5 Ibid., 201.
6 Ibid., 207, 210.
7 *1907 Class Book.*
8 Mary Schenck Woolman, *The Making of a Girls Trade School* (New York: Columbia University Press, 1909), 2, 10. The study appeared after *The Survey* article was published, but Louise did her research at the Manhattan Trade School for Girls and was familiar with its goals and principles.
9 Ibid., 43.
10 Odencrantz, "The Irregularity of Employment," May 1909, 210.
11 *Columbia University Bulletin,* 1907.
12 Ibid.
13 *1907 Class Book.*
14 *Social Welfare History Project* (2011), http://socialwelfare.library.vcu.edu/people/devine-edward-t-3/; Devine was co-founder of the National Child Labor Committee and editor of *The Survey,* which published Louise's M.A. thesis.
15 *Columbia University Bulletin,* 1907.
16 Davis, 245.
17 Domenica Barbuto, *American Settlement Houses and Progressive Social Reform* (Phoenix: Oryx Press, 1999), ix.
18 Ryan Brubacher, "Focusing on Lewis Hine's Photographic Technique," January 31, 2019, https://blogs.loc.gov/picturethis/2019/01/focusing-on-lewis-hines-photographic-technique.

Chapter V

1. For accounts of the strike, see Tyler Anbinder, *City of Dreams* (Boston and New York: Houghton Mifflin Harcourt, 2016), 431-33; Dennis von Drehle, *Triangle: the Fire that Changed America* (New York: Atlantic Monthly Press, 2003), 6-17; Mike Wallace, *Greater Gotham, A History of New York City from 1898 to 1919* (New York: Oxford University Press, 2017), 708-717.
2. Ruth Crocker, *Mrs. Russell Sage: Women's Activism and Philanthropy in the Gilded Age and Progressive Era America* (Bloomington: Indiana University Press, 2006), 226.
3. David Hammack and Stanton Wheeler, *Social Science in the Making. Essays on the Russell Sage Foundation, 1907–1972* (New York: Russell Sage Foundation, 1995), 3, 26.
4. John Glenn et al., *Russsell Sage Foundation 1907-1946, Vol. One* (New York: Russell Sage Foundation, 1947), 61.
5. Richards, "Projections," 8.
6. Quoted in Charlene Haddock Seigfried, *Pragmatism and Feminism. Reweaving the Social Fabric* (Chicago: Chicago University Press, 1996), 37.
7. Mary Van Kleeck, *Women in the Bookbinding Trade* (New York: Russell Sage Foundation), 1913, 4.
8. Ibid., 6.
9. Ibid., 147-48.
10. *New York Times*, March 26, 1911.
11. Kirstin Downey, *The Woman behind the New Deal* (New York: Random House, 2009), 36.
12. Van Kleeck, *Bookbinding Trade*, 36.
13. Ibid., 11.
14. Cynthia Enloe, *The Curious Feminist.* (Berkeley: University of California Press, 2004), 3, 5.
15. Van Kleeck, *Bookbinding Trade*, 53.
16. Ibid., 154, 155.
17. *1907 Class Book.*
18. Van Kleeck, *Bookbinding Trade*, 48.
19. Ibid., 49, 146.
20. Ibid., 143.
21. Ibid., 84, 86.
22. Ibid., 228-29; https:// teachingamericanhistory.org/library/document/progressive-platform-of-1912, accessed 1/11/2021.
23. Mary Van Kleeck, *A Seasonal Industry. A Study of the Millinery Trade in New York* (New York: Russell Sage Foundation, 1917), 26-27.
24. Ibid., 7.

25 Ibid., 14.
26 Ibid., 26, 171, 179.
27 Letter to John Glenn, May 11, 1912, Russell Sage Foundation Archives.
28 Mary Van Kleeck, *Industrial Investigations of the Russell Sage Foundation* (New York: Russell Sage Foundation, 1915), 3.
29 Cited in David C. Hammack and Stanton Wheeler, *Social Science in the Making, Essays on the Russell Sage Foundation, 1907–1972* (New York: Russell Sage Foundation, 1995), 24.
30 Van Kleeck, *Industrial Investigations*, 4.
31 Van Kleeck, *Bookbinding Trade*, 235-36.
32 Mary Van Kleeck, *Artificial Flower Makers* (New York: Russell Sage Foundation, 1913), 8.
33 Ibid., vi.
34 Van Kleeck, *Artificial Flower Makers*, 228-31.
35 Ibid.
36 Mary Van Kleeck, *Working Girls in Evening Schools* (New York: Russell Sage Foundation, 1914), 18.
37 Ibid., 23.
38 Ibid., 24.
39 Ibid., 25. *1907 Classbook*.
40 Van Kleeck, *Evening Schools*, 123.
41 Ibid., 180-81.
42 Ibid., 59. In a *Washington Post* column on diversity and inclusion, October 18, 2018, former CEO Carly Fiorina observed, "When talent is squandered, when human potential is crushed, when someone's spirit is broken, we all lose. ... [We] have plenty of work to do that can make a real difference."

Chapter VI

1 *Class Notes,* 1912.
2 Van Kleeck, *Evening Schools,* 9; letter to John Glenn, May 11, 1912 (Russell Sage Foundation Archives).
3 Letter to John Glenn, May 11, 1912.
4 Ibid.
5 Ibid. and memorandum to John Glenn dated October 6, 1911. (Both mention a study of the dressmaking trade, which seems to have been abandoned as a separate project or incorporated into the Italian study; no title containing "dressmaking" appears in the Foundation's list of publications); Downey, 29.
6 Odencrantz, *Italian Women in Industry* (New York: Russell Sage Foundation, 1919), 10-11.

7   Ibid., 3-4.
8   Ibid., 8.
9   Ibid.
10 Ibid., 5.
11 Ibid., 12.
12 Ibid., 31-32.
13 Ibid., 68.
14 Ibid., 68-74.
15 Ibid., 126.
16 Ibid., 151.
17 Ibid., 106-07; this is probably not the same girl that Louise had interviewed for the millinery study, whose trade was flower-making (see page 85 above); the name Theresa is common.
18 Ibid., 95, 97.
19 Ibid., 123-24.
20 Ibid., 110-11.
21 *1907 Class Book*; Odencrantz, *Italian Women*, 14-15.
22 *1907 Class Book*.
23 Odencrantz, *Italian Women*, 225-26, 201.
24 L.P. Ayres, *Laggards in Our Schools* (New York: Russell Sage Foundation, 1909), cited Odencrantz, *Italian Women*, 257.
25 Odencrantz, *Italian Women*, 254.
26 Ibid., 258, 259.
27 Ibid., 262.
28 Ibid., 119.
29 Ibid., 176.
30 Ibid., 176, 179.
31 *1907 Class Book*.
32 Odencrantz, *Italian Women*, 26, 28, 30.
33 Ibid., 285-86.
34 Ibid., 240, 222.
35 Ibid., 2-3.
36 Ibid., 289-90.
37 Ibid., 292-94.
38 Ibid., 296.
39 Sophonisba Breckenridge, "Italian Women in Industry: A Study of Conditions in New York City," *Journal of Political Economy* 27, no. 6 (June, 1919): 520.
40 Annie Marion Maclean, "*Italian Women in Industry*. Louise C. Odencrantz," *American Journal of Sociology* 26, no. 5 (March, 1921): 657-58.
41 Cf. Miriam Cohen, *Workshop to Office: Two Generations of Italian Women in New York City, 1900-1950* (Ithaca: Cornell University Press, 2014);

Edvige Giunta and Joseph Sciorra, *Embroidered Stories: Interpreting Women's Domestic Needlework from the Italian Diaspora* (Jackson: University of Mississippi Press, 2014); and Laura Hapke, *Sweatshop: The History of an American Idea* (New Brunswick: Rutgers University Press, 2004).

Chapter VII

1 Louise C. Odencrantz and Zenas L Potter, *Industrial Conditions in Springfield, Illinois* (New York: Russell Sage Foundation, 1916), 5.
2 Ibid., 7; "Franklin Roosevelt's Statement on the National Industrial Recovery Act," *Franklin D. Roosevelt Presidential Library and Museum Our Documents*. June 16, 1933.
3 Odencrantz and Potter, 11-36.
4 Ibid., 11-12, 27.
5 Ibid., 111
6 Ibid., 25, 23.
7 Ibid., 136.
8 Ibid., 118, 128-29.
9 Ibid., 40, 109.
10 Ibid., 123.
11 Ibid., 119.
12 Ibid., 60.
13 Ibid., 56-58.
14 Ibid., 127.
15 Christopher Lasch, *Haven in a Heartless World* (New York: Basic Books, 1977), 12-13.
16 Odencrantz and Potter, 57.
17 Ibid., 141.
18 Ibid., 143.
19 Shelby M. Harrison, *Social Conditions in an American City. A Summary of the Findings of the Springfield Survey,* vol. 3 (New York: Russell Sage Foundation, 1918-1920), 12.
20 Vachel Lindsay, "Father Springfield in the Mirror. Survey and Exhibition of Springfield Illinois under the Direction of Russell Sage Foundation with Local and National Cooperation." *The Survey*, XXXIII (December 12, 1914): 316.
21 Ibid.
22 Odencrantz and Potter, 90.
23 Lindsay, "Father Springfield," 316.
24 Ibid.

Chapter VIII

1. Richards, "Projections," 9.
2. Ibid.
3. Ibid.
4. Ibid.
5. Odencrantz and Potter, 98.
6. Ray Lubove, *The Struggle for Social Security* (Pittsburgh: University of Pittsburgh Press, 1986), 155-56.
7. Charles B. Barnes, "Public Bureaus of Employment" in *The Annals of the American Academy of Political and Social Sciences*, 59, (May 1915): 186, 190.
8. "New State Employment Bureau Attracts Hundreds," *New York Herald*, January 10, 1915, Odencrantz Papers, folder 16.
9. *Sunday Tribune*, April 2, 1916, Odencrantz Papers, folder 16.
10. "Trained and Untrained Women Apply to State Employment Bureau for Work," *Brooklyn Daily Eagle*, March 7, 1915, Odencrantz Papers, folder 16.
11. Ibid.
12. "Finding Work for Women through the State Public Employment Office," *New York Sunday Call*, December 13, 1915, Odencrantz Papers, folder 16.
13. *New York Tribune*, November 1, 1916, Odencrantz Papers, folder 16.
14. *New York Sunday Call*, December 13, 1915, Odencrantz Papers, folder 16.
15. Odencrantz, "State's First Employment Bureau a Success," *New York Times*, March 12, 1916. Capitalization of "public employment bureau" is inconsistent in the text of the article.
16. Ibid.
17. Odencrantz, "How I Discovered Myself," *Evening Journal*, January 22, 1916, Odencrantz Papers, folder 16.
18. Carolyn Heilbrun, *Writing a Woman's Life* (New York: Ballantine Books, 1988), 24.
19. "How I Discovered Myself"; Putnam quoted in Duer Miller, 36.
20. Odencrantz, "How I Discovered Myself;" Odencrantz and Potter, *Industrial Conditions*, 96.
21. Richards, "Projections," 9.
22. Ibid.; "Urges a Children's Bureau: Miss Odencrantz Wants State to Create Separate Employment Agency," *Evening Post*, April 4, 1916, Odencrantz Papers, folder 16.
23. Odencrantz, "Why Jennie Hates Flowers," *World Outlook* (October 1917): 12-13.

24 Alice Kessler-Harris, *Out to Work* (Oxford: Oxford University Press, 1983), 219.
25 *Annual Report of the New York State Industrial Commission* transmitted to the legislature April 11, 1918, 230-31.
26 "Chance for Middle-Aged Women in Ranks of City Wage Earners." *Brooklyn Daily Eagle*, September 11, 1917, Odencrantz Papers, folder 16.
27 *Annual Report*, 1918, 235; *NAACP: A Century in the Fight for Freedom*, accessed through https://www.loc.gov/exhibits/naacp/founding-and-early-years.html.
28 Hilda Lomes, *Woman's National Farm and Garden Association Bulletin*, vol. 6, issue 6 (December 1918).
29 *Barnard Bulletin*, cited in Elaine Weiss, *Fruits of Victory: The Woman's Land Army of America in the Great War* (Washington, D.C.: Potomac Books, 2008), 54; Odencrantz, "From Factory to Field, (*Association Monthly*, March 1918): 98 (accessed on-line at https://compass.five-colleges.edu/object/smith:358222). The same issue contains an article by Florence Kelley, "From Field to Factory" (80-81), which concludes "For migrant colored girls two especially urgent needs are intelligent organization and adequate training in skill." The matching titles suggests that both articles were part of an ongoing debate.
30 Weiss, 215, 216.
31 "Farmerettes Win Warm Praise," *Evening Sun*, June 21, 1918, Odencrantz Papers, folder 16.
32 Odencrantz, "From Factory to Field," *Association Monthly*, 99.
33 *Opportunities for War Time Training for Women in New York City, 1918-1919* (New York: Clearing House for War Time Training for Women, 1918), 4.
34 Ibid., 16, 5.
35 Ibid., 10.
36 "Methods and Results of Training Women for Industry," speech on May 19, 1919 at State University of Albany Educational Congress, typescript, Odencrantz Papers, folder 4.
37 "War not to End Labor Control," *Evening Sun*, November 4, 1918, Odencrantz Papers, folder 16.
38 "Calls Women to Fill 'Aching Void' in War Factories," *New York Tribune*, November 2, 1918, Odencrantz Papers, folder 16.
39 "Woman's Future in Industry," *Evening Sun*, November 14, 1918, Odencrantz Papers, folder 16.
40 Kessler-Harris, 224.
41 "Blissful Days Ahead for Business Men when 'Gem Girl' Stenographers Return," *New York Evening Telegram*, November 19, 1918, Odencrantz Papers, folder 16.

42 "Women Face New Labor Conditions," *Evening Post*, January 27, 1919, Odencrantz Papers, folder 16.
43 Glenn, *Russell Sage Foundation 1907-1946*, 358.
44 *Evening Post*, March 25, 1919, Odencrantz Papers, folder 16.
45 Michael McGerr, *A Fierce Discontent: The Rise and Fall of the Progressive Movement, 1870-1920* (New York: Simon & Schuster, 2003), xvi, 302-04.
46 Cf. Walter Nugent, *Progressivism: A Very Short Introduction* (Oxford: Oxford University Press, 2010), 124: "While the federal government turned conservative, the social-justice, educational, and local-government Progressives found plenty to do."

Chapter IX

1 "Work Resume," Odencrantz Papers, folder 1.
2 Guy Alchon, *The Invisible Hand of Planning* (Princeton: Princeton University Press, 1985), 45. See also Alchon, "Mary Van Kleeck and Scientific Management" in Daniel Nelson, ed., *A Mental Revolution: Scientific Management since Taylor* (Columbus: Ohio University Press, 1992).
3 Odencrantz, "Public Employment Service from the Point of View of an Employment Manager," *International Association of Public Employment Services, Proceedings of Eighth Annual Meeting, Ottawa, Canada, September 20-22* (Department of Labour, Ottowa, 1921), 64-65.
4 Steve Golin, *The Fragile Bridge: Paterson Silk Strike 1913* (Philadelphia: Temple University Press, 1988), 23.
5 Ibid., 24.
6 See Madelyn Shaw, "For your Easter bonnet: Silk ribbons," americanhistory.si.edu/blog/easter-ribbons, April 13, 2017.
7 Golin, 190.
8 *Barnard Bulletin*, March 5, 1920.
9 Margaret Gadsby, "Trade Agreement in the Silk Industry of New York City, in *Bulletin of the United States Bureau of Labor Statistics, Issue 341* (Washington, D.C.: Government Printing Office, 1923), 1.
10 Letter dated April 30, 1920 in Van Kleeck Papers, Smith College Archives, box 101, folder 9.
11 Gadsby, 7-8.
12 Anon., "The Impartial Chairman in Silk Ribbon Trade," *The American Silk Journal*, 40, no. 1 (January 1921): 54, 66.
13 Louise C. Odencrantz, "Employment Management and the Silk Industry," *The American Silk Journal*, 40, no. 12, (December 1921): 58, Odencrantz Papers, folder 7.
14 Gadsby, 3.
15 See *Silk and Manufacturers of Silk*, published by United States Tariff

Commission (Washington, D.C.: Government Printing Office, 1918), 103.
16 Odencrantz, "Employment Management and the Silk Industry," 57, 60.
17 Gadsby, 48.
18 Gadsby, 55.
19 Odencrantz, "Employment Management and the Silk Industry," 60.
20 *Silk*, XIV, no. 10 (October 1921): 48.
21 Louise Odencrantz, "Common Sense in Industry: How Silk Ribbons are Manufactured without Strikes or Lockouts," *The Metropolis*, June 1, 1921, Odencrantz Papers, folder 7.
22 "Eating in the Factory," *The American Silk Journal*, 40, no. 3 (March 1921): 91; advertisements appeared in various 1921 issues of the journal.
23 Odencrantz, Louise. "Industrial Welfare Work," *The Survey*, 48 (1922): 631, Odencrantz Papers, folder 9.
24 Odencrantz, Louise. "Personnel Work in America," *Personnel Administration*, 10, no. 4 (August 1922): 8, Odencrantz Papers, folder 4.
25 Ibid., 14.
26 Odencrantz, Louise. "Industrial Welfare Work," *The Survey*, 48 (1922): 631.
27 Guy Alchon "Mary Van Kleeck and Scientific Management," in Daniel Nelson, ed., *A Mental Revolution* (Columbus, Ohio: Ohio State University Press, 1992), 109.
28 Odencrantz, "The Place of Personnel Work in a Business Organization," typescript of speech given October 9, 1922, to New Haven Industrial Relations Council, Odencrantz Papers, folder 4.
29 "Personnel Work in Factories," *Public Health Nurse,* XV August 1923: 395, 396, Odencrantz Papers, folder 5.
30 Gadsby, 50-51, 54.

Chapter X

1 Downey, 59.
2 Susan Ware, *Beyond Suffrage: Women in the New Deal* (Cambridge: Harvard University Press, 1981), 26.
3 Undated letter in family archive; Louise attended the Cambridge conference of the IRI in the summer of 1928.
4 Letter dated September 17, 1930, family archive.
5 Documents Related to Estate of Frederikke Odencrantz, family archive.
6 Ware, 2.

7   Perkins cited in John Louis Recchiuti, *Civic Engagement: Social Science and Progressive-Era Reform in New York City* (Philadelphia: University of Pennsylvania Press, 2006), 7; Ware, 33.
8   Guy Alchon, "Mary Van Kleeck and Social-Economic Planning," *Journal of Policy History*, 3, no.1 (1991): 14.
9   Letters in Mary van Kleeck Papers, Sophia Smith Collection, Smith College, Northampton, Mass., box 101, folder 9.
10 "Gossip," *The Survey*, vol. 62 (April 15, 1929), Odencrantz Papers, folder 14.
11 Ruth Reticker, 1956 Christmas letter to friends, in family archive.
12 "The Rubber Plant" in family archive.
13 Ware, 29.
14 Ruth Oldenziel, "Gender and Scientific Management, Women and the History of the International Institute for Industrial Relations, 1922-1946," *Journal of Management History*, 6, no. 7 (2000): 324-325; Benny Carlson "The IRI and Its Swedish Connection," *American Studies in Scandinavia*, 39, 2007: 18.
15 Odencrantz, "The International Industrial Welfare and Personnel Congress, Holland, June 19-26, 1925," *Bulletin of the Taylor Society* (October 1925): 231-32; Odencrantz also reported on the conference in *American Management Review*, November 1925, 341-43.
16 Odencrantz, Congress of the International Industrial Relations Association," *The Compass*, published by the American Association of Social Workers, July-Aug. 1928 Vol. IX: 3-4. See also Odencrantz, "Cambridge Congress of the I.R.I." in *The Personnel Journal* (October 1928): 226-35.
17 Oldenziel, 326.

Chapter XI

1   Mary van Kleeck and Graham Romeyn Taylor, *The Annals of the American Academy of Political and Social Science*, 101 (1922): 168.
2   David C. Hammack and Stanton Wheeler, *Social Science in the Making: Essays on the Russell Sage Foundation, 1907-1972* (New York: Russell Sage Foundation, 1995), 19.
3   Ellen Agnew, *From Charity to Social Work: Mary E. Richmond and the Creation of an American Profession* (Urbana: University of Illinois Press, 2005), 5.
4   Mary Richmond, *Social Diagnosis* (New York: Russell Sage Foundation, 1917), 379.
5   Agnew, 168.

6 Daniel Walkowitz, *Working with Class: Social Workers and the Politics of Middle-Class Identity* (Chapel Hill: University of North Carolina Press, 1999), 59.
7 Louise Odencrantz, *The Social Worker in Family, Medical and Psychiatric Social Work* (New York: Harper & Brothers, 1929), 2-3.
8 Odencrantz, 6.
9 Agnew, 7.
10 Odencrantz, 9.
11 Odencrantz, 117.
12 Odencrantz, 263.
13 Odencrantz, 5.
14 Mary Antoinette Cannon, *Hospital Social Work*, New York School of Social Work; Frank Bruno review in *The Compass* X (April 1929): 8; Walkowitz, 59.
15 Kim E. Nielsen, *A Disability History of the United States*. (Boston: Beacon Press, 2012), 100.
16 Mary La Dame, *Securing Employment for the Handicapped: A Study of Placement Agencies for This Group in New York City* (New York: Welfare Council of New York City, 1927) 35.
17 "Work Resumé, " Odencrantz Papers, folder 1.
18 "How I Discovered Myself—Another Successful Woman Tells of Her Work," *Evening Journal,* January 22, 1916, Odencrantz Papers, folder 16.
19 Odencrantz, "The Employment Problem of the Physically Handicapped," presented at the State Conference of Social Work, Albany, New York, 1929; reprinted in *Hospital Social Service*, XXI, 1930: 463-70, Odencrantz Papers, folder 5.
20 Ibid.
21 La Dame, 22.
22 Odencrantz, "Medical Work in Industrial Medicine and Traumatic Surgery," presented to the American College of Surgeons, New York, in October 1931, Odencrantz Papers, folder 5.
23 Ibid.
24 Odencrantz, *How Physically Handicapped People Find Work. A Manual of Placement Procedure* (published by the New York State Department of Labor, 1935), 28, Odencrantz Papers, folder 17.
25 Odencrantz, "Occupational Therapy and the Placement of the Handicapped in Industry," *Occupational Therapy and Rehabilitation"* (June 1934): 189-95, Odencrantz Papers, folder 5.
26 Peter Catapano and Rosemarie Garland-Thomsen, *About Us: Essays from The New York Times Disability Series* (New York: New York Times, 2019), Introduction.

27 Letter to the Editor, *New York Times,* July 22, 1929; reference to Steinmetz quoted in Donald Harrington's eulogy May 25,1969.
28 Nielsen, 105.
29 Odencrantz, "An Address by the Fairer Sex," *Spokes in the Wheel of the Rotary Club of New York* 18, no. 26 (October 28, 1930): 2, Odencrantz Papers, folder 16.
30 Rosemarie Garland-Thomsen, "Becoming Disabled," *New York Times,* August 19, 2016.
31 Katherine Kish Sklar and Beverly Wilson Palmer, eds, *The Selected Letters of Florence Kelley* (Urbana: University of Illinois Press, 2009), 464-65.
32 Josephine Goldmark *Impatient Crusader: Florence Kelley's Life Story* (Urbana: University of Illinois Press. 1953), 111.
33 These events were reported in the *New York Times* on July 9, 1931 and January 9, 1935.
34 Governor's Commission on Unemployment Relief, *The Public Employment Services in the State of New York* (Albany, 1935), 39.
35 Richards, "Projections," 10.
36 Ibid.

Chapter XII

1 "34 Social Agencies Seek Aid. Miss Odencrantz Urges Industries to Help in Providing Work," *New York Times,* July 23, 1928.
2 Frances Perkins, *The Roosevelt that I Knew* (New York: Viking Press, 1946), 92.
3 Letter dated June 10, 1929, Odencrantz Papers, folder 3; "Picks 28 to Survey State Job Agencies," *New York Times,* June 14, 1929.
4 Quoted in *The Public Employment Services in the State of New York* (Albany, J. B. Lyon company, printers, 1935), 21. The 1929 *Times* article cited above lists Arthur Young of Industrial Relations Counselors as chair of the committee; the report lists Mary La Dame (whom Louise knew from the Russell Sage Foundation Department of Industrial Studies) as chair.
5 "Finds Employment Fair. R.A. Flinn Sees No Cause for Alarm Here in the Situation," *New York Times,* November 19, 1929.
6 Figures cited on website: https://blogs.baruch.cuny.edu/his1000summer2011/2011/07/04/the-great-depression-2/.
7 "Thousands Face Starvation if Relief is not Restored," *New York Times,* January 11, 1932.
8 "Federal Job Board Names 50 Advisers," *New York Times,* August 13, 1933.

9 Downey, 232.
10 "Work Resume," Odencrantz Papers, folder 1.
11 Unpublished manuscript shared with Esther Peterson, Odencrantz Papers, folder 15.
12 Mary Van Kleeck, "A planned Economy as a National Objective for Social Work," *The Compass* (May 1933): 23. See also Guy Alchon, "Mary Van Kleeck and Scientific Management," in Daniel Nelson, ed., *A Mental Revolution*, 102-29.
13 Unpublished manuscript shared with Esther Peterson, Odencrantz Papers, folder 15.
14 The cartoon appeared in the *New York World*. Louise's copy is undated.
15 New York (State) Governor's Commission on Unemployment Relief, *The Administration of Home Relief In New York City: Submitted to Governor Herbert H. Lehman, June 24, 1935* (Albany: J. B. Lyon Company, 1935), 21.
16 Ibid.
17 Ibid., 18-20.
18 Raymond C. Atkinson, Louise C. Odencrantz, and Ben Deming, *Public Employment Service in the United States* (Chicago: Public Administration Service, 1938), vi.
19 Ibid. 273.
20 Ibid., 279, 297.
21 Ibid., 328, 311.
22 Review of "Public Employment Service in the United States," *Social Service Review*, Vol. 13, no. 4, (December 1939): 719.
23 "Labor Office Sets up a Board of Appeals," *New York Times*, September 26, 1937.
24 "Job Fund Inquiry Scores Officials," *New York Times*, March 16, 1939.
25 "Minutes: Welfare Council, Committee on Training, 1935-1937," Odencrantz Papers, folder 19.
26 Odencrantz, "Recent Developments in Employment Services," *Occupations: The Vocational Guidance Journal*, January 1940, vol. 8: 249-53, Odencrantz Papers, folder 5.

Chapter XIII

1 Introduction to Frederikke's unpublished memoirs in family archive.
2 Vera Brittain, *Testament of Youth* (reprint London: Virago Press, 1980), 117.
3 Odencrantz, "These Jobs Beg for Workers," in *Survey Mid-Monthly*, 34 (September 1945): 219-21, Odencrantz Papers, folder 5. U.S. Bureau of

Labor Statistics, *Occupational Outlook Handbook,* Social Workers 2020 Median Pay. www.bls.gov/ooh/community-and-social-service/social-workers.htm, accessed September 22, 2021,
4 Ibid.
5 David Walkowitz, *Working with Class: Social Workers and the Politics of Middle-Class Identity*, (Chapel Hill: University of North Carolina Press, 1999), 188.
6 Hoffer, Joe R. "Toward a Progressive Vocational Service for Social Work." *The Compass* 28, no. 6, (September 1947): 5.
7 Crosby's announcement is cited in "Notes and Comments," *Social Service Review,* 23, (June 1949): 232.
8 *Survey Mid-Monthly* 32, no. 1 (January 1947): 27.
9 Marion O. Robinson, *A World Mutual Service; a Common Quest* (Washington, D.C.: National Board of the Young Women's Christian Association of the U.S.A., 1973), 14-15.
10 "About YWCA: History." Accessed June 21, 2019. https://www.ywca.org/about/history.
11 Letters to Danish relative, Bodil Jessen, dated January 13 and May 24, 1959.
12 Eleanor Roosevelt, "My Day, October 11, 1952," *The Eleanor Roosevelt Papers Digital Edition* (2017), accessed 2/22/2020, https://www2.gwu.edu/~erpapers/myday/displaydoc.cfm?_y=1952&_f=md002350.
13 Letter to Marianne Hesseldahl, dated October 18, 1952.
14 H.M. James, "The Sixth International Conference of Social Work Held at Madras, December 12th-19th, 1952," *Australian Journal of Social Work,* 5, no. 2 (1953): 274, 275.
15 L.S. Kudchedkar, "World Social Workers Meet," *Indian Journal of Social Work,* 13 (1952-53): 274, 278.
16 Kudchedkar, 276.
17 *Barnard Bulletin,* December 10, 1953.
18 Ibid., March 8, 1951.
19 "Over 35? Housewife? No Experience?" *Barnard College Alumnae Monthly* (February 1952): 15.
20 "Social Work Opportunities—A Practical Appraisal of the Field for Mature Women," *Barnard College Alumnae Monthly,* January 1957, 17-19.
21 "Five-Year Classes Celebrate Reunion, *Barnard College Alumnae Monthly* (July 1957): 15.

Chapter XIV

1. Letter to Bodil Jessen dated January 19, 1961.
2. Death notice for Louise Brewer, *New York Times*, October 21, 1997.
3. Letters to Bodil Jessen dated February 9, 1962 and November 22, 1966.
4. Letters to Bodil Jessen dated January 11 and May 7, 1968.
5. Letters to Bodil Jessen dated April 18, 1968, November 26, 1968 and January 20, 1969.
6. Letter to Marguerite, dated March 15, 1969.
7. "Louise C. Odencrantz Is Dead. Advocate of Jobs for Women," *New York Times,* April 9, 1969.

Epilogue

1. Memorial Service for Louise C. Odencrantz, May 25, 1969, typescript.

Bibliography

Books by Louise Odencrantz

Industrial Conditions in Springfield, Illinois (with Zenas Potter). New York: Russell Sage Foundation, 1916.
Italian Women in Industry; a Study of Conditions in New York City. New York: Russsell Sage Foundation, 1919; re-issued New York: Arno Press, 1977.
The Social Worker in Family, Medical and Psychiatric Social Work. New York: Harper & Brothers, 1929.
Public Employment Service in the United States (with Raymond C. Atkinson and Ben Deming). Chicago: Committee on Public Administration of the Social Science Research Council by Public Administration Service, 1938.

Works Cited

Agnew, Ellen. *From Charity to Social Work: Mary E. Richmond and the Creation of an American Profession.* Urbana: University of Illinois Press, 2005.
Alchon, Guy. *The Invisible Hand of Planning.* Princeton: Princeton University Press, 1985.
Alchon, Guy. "Mary Van Kleeck and Social-Economic Planning." *Journal of Policy History,* 6 (January 1991), 1-23.
Anbinder, Tyler. *City of Dreams.* Boston and New York: Houghton Mifflin Harcourt, 2016.
Annual Report of the New York State Industrial Commission. Transmitted to the legislature April 11, 1918. Albany: State Department of Labor, 1918.
Barbuto, Domenica. *American Settlement Houses and Progressive Social Reform.* Phoenix: Oryx Press, 1999.
Barnes, Charles B. "Public Bureaus of Employment." *Annals of the American Academy of Political and Social Sciences,* 59 (May 1915): 185-93.
Carlson, Benny. "The IRI and Its Swedish Connection." *American Studies in Scandinavia,* 39 (2007): 13-32.

Catapano, Peter and Garland-Thomsen, Rosemarie. *About Us: Essays from The New York Times Disability Series*. New York: New York Times, 2019.

Clark, John Bates. *The Distribution of Wealth: A Theory of Wages, Interest and Profits*. New York: The Macmillan Company, 1899.

Davis, Allen F. *Spearheads for Reform, The Social Settlements and the Progressive Movement, 1890-1914*. New Brunswick: Rutgers University Press, 1984.

Downey, Kirstin. *The Woman behind the New Deal*. New York: Random House, 2009.

Duer-Miller, Alice. *Barnard College—the First Fifty Years*. New York: Columbia University Press, 1939.

Enloe, Cynthia. *The Curious Feminist*. Berkeley: University of California Press, 2004.

Gadsby, Margaret. "Trade Agreement in the Silk Industry of New York City." *Bulletin of the United States Bureau of Labor Statistics, 341*. Washington, D.C.: Government Printing Office, 1923.

Glenn, John M., et al. *Russell Sage Foundation 1907-1946*. New York: Russell Sage Foundation, 1947.

Golin, Steve. *The Fragile Bridge: Paterson Silk Strike 1913*. Philadelphia: Temple University Press, 1988.

Goldmark, Josephine. *Fatigue and Efficiency*. New York: Russell Sage Foundation, 1912.

Goldmark, Josephine. *Impatient Crusader: Florence Kelley's Life Story*. Urbana: University of Illinois Press, 1953.

Governor's Commission on Unemployment Relief. *The Public Employment Services in the State of New York*. Albany: State Department of Labor, 1935.

Hammack, David C. and Wheeler, Stanton. *Social Science in the Making: Essays on the Russell Sage Foundation, 1907-1972*. New York: Russell Sage Foundation, 1995.

Harrison, Shelby M. *The Springfield Survey: A Study of Social Conditions in an American City*. New York: Russell Sage Foundation, 1914-1920.

Heilbrun, Carolyn, *Writing a Woman's Life*. New York: Ballantine Books, 1988.

Hermalyn, Gary. *Morris High School and the Creation of the New York City Public High School System*. New York: The Bronx County Historical Society, 1995.

Hoffer, Joe R. "Toward a Progressive Vocational Service for Social Work." *The Compass* 28, no. 6. (September 1947): 3-27.

James, H.M. "The Sixth International Conference of Social Work Held in Madras, December 12th-19th." *Australian Journal of Social Work*, 6 (1953): 252-78.

Kessler-Harris, Alice. *Out to Work*. Oxford: Oxford University Press, 1983.
Kudchedkar, L.S. "World Social Workers Meet." *Indian Journal of Social Work*, 13 (1952-53): 270-79.
La Dame, Mary. *Securing Employment for the Handicapped: A Study of Placement Agencies for This Group in New York City*. New York: Welfare Council of New York City, 1927.
Lasch, Christopher. *Haven in a Heartless World*. New York: Basic Books, 1977.
Lindsay, Vachel. "Father Springfield in the Mirror. Survey and Exhibition of Springfield Illinois under the Direction of Russell Sage Foundation with Local and National Cooperation." *The Survey*, 23 (December 12, 1914): 316-18.
Lubove, Ray. *The Struggle for Social Security*. Pittsburgh: University of Pittsburgh Press, 1986.
McGerr, Michael. *A Fierce Discontent: The Rise and Fall of the Progressive Movement, 1870-1920*. New York: Simon & Schuster, 2003.
Nelson, Daniel, ed. *A Mental Revolution: Scientific Management since Taylor*. Columbus: Ohio State University Press, 1992.
Nielsen, Kim E. *A Disability History of the United States*. Boston: Beacon Press, 2012.
Nugent, Walter. *Progressivism: A Very Short Introduction*. Oxford: Oxford University Press, 2010.
Oldenziel, Ruth. "Gender and Scientific Management, Women and the History of the International Institute for Industrial Relations, 1922-1946." *Journal of Management History*, 66 (2000): 323-42.
Perkins, Frances. *The Roosevelt I Knew*. New York: Viking Press, 1946.
Recchiuti, John Louis. *Civic Engagement: Social Science and Progressive-Era Reform in New York City*. Philadelphia: University of Pennsylvania Press, 2006.
Richmond, Mary. *Social Diagnosis*. New York: Russell Sage Foundation, 1917.
Robinson, Marion O. *A World Mutual Service; a Common Quest*. New York: National Board of the Young Women's Christian Association of the U.S.A., 1973.
Rosenberg, Rosalind. *Changing the Subject, How the Women of Columbia Shaped the Way We Think about Sex and Politics*. New York: Columbia University Press, 2004.
Seager, Henry Rogers. *Social Insurance: A Program of Social Reform*. New York: Macmillan, 1910.
Sklar, Katherine Kish and Beverly Wilson Palmer, eds. *The Selected Letters of Florence Kelley*. Champaign: University of Illinois Press, 2009.
United States Tariff Commission. *Silk and Manufacturers of Silk*. Washington, D.C.: Government Printing Office, 1918.

Van Kleeck, Mary. *Women in the Bookbinding Trade*. New York: Russell Sage Foundation, 1913.

Van Kleeck, Mary. *Artificial Flower Makers*. New York: Russell Sage Foundation, 1913.

Van Kleeck, Mary. *Working Girls in Evening Schools*. New York: Russell Sage Foundation, 1914.

Van Kleeck, Mary. *A Seasonal Industry: A Study of the Millinery Trade in New York*. New York: Russell Sage Foundation, 1917.

Van Kleeck, Mary and Taylor, Graham Romeyn. "The Professional Organization of Social Work." *The Annals of the American Academy of Political and Social Science*, 101 (1922): 158-68.

Walkowitz, David. *Working with Class: Social Workers and the Politics of Middle-Class Identity*. Chapel Hill: University of North Carolina Press, 1999.

Wallace, Mike. *Greater Gotham, A History of New York City from 1898 to 1919*. New York: Oxford University Press, 2017.

Ware, Susan. *Beyond Suffrage: Women in the New Deal*. Cambridge: Harvard University Press, 1981.

Weiss, Elaine. *Fruits of Victory: The Woman's Land Army of America in the Great War*. Washington, D.C.: Potomac Books, 2008.

White, Marian Churchill. *History of Barnard*. New York: Columbia University Press, 1954.

Woods, Robert A. and Kennedy, Albert J., eds. *Handbook of Settlements*. New York: Russell Sage Foundation, 1911.

Woolman, Mary Schenck. *The Making of a Girls Trade School*. New York: Columbia University Press, 1909.

Archives

Barnard College Archives, https://archives.barnard.edu.

Louise C. Odencrantz Papers, 1909-1968; MC 195. Schlesinger Library, Radcliffe Institute, Harvard University, Cambridge, Mass. https://id.lib.harvard.edu/ead/sch00834/catalog.

New York Times Article Archive /www.nytimes.com.

Russell Sage Foundation Archives, Rockefeller Archive Center.

Sophia Smith Collection of Women's History, Smith College.

Family archives held by Todd Stockbauer and Nana Rinehart

Index

Abbott, Grace, 145
Addams, Jane, 4, 35, 57, 102, 167
Alliance Employment Bureau, 34, 36, 42, 46
Amalgamated Textile Workers, 114
American College of Surgeons, 142
Americans with Disabilities Act, 145
American Association of Social Workers (AASW), 135, 139
Anderson, Mary, 146
Atkinson, Ben, 155
Ayres, Leonard, 67

Barnard College, 1, 2, 21, 26, 29-37, 52, 67, 99, 102-03, 113, 147, 165, 170
Barnes, Charles, 94, 95, 107, 115, 124
Bergstrom, Olof, 8
Bowles, Chester, 168
Brandeis, Louis, 59, 126
Brewer, Louise, 174
Brewster, William, 31

Cadbury, Dorothy, 132
Chicago, 22, 35, 80
child labor, 4, 33, 34, 57, 60, 63
Clark, John Bates, 32
Clearing House for War Time Training for Women, 104, 140
College Settlement, Rivington Street, 2, 5, 35, 36, 38, 39-47, 74, 94, 150

Columbia University, 2, 26, 30, 31, 36, 38, 42, 44, 45, 50, 51, 167, 170, 176
Committee on Vocational Guidance, 100
Committee on Women's Work, 46, 47, 50, 51, 60, 67, 69, 83
Crosby, Helen, 165

Dabringhaus, Gustav, 132
Deming, Richard, 155
Denmark, 10, 18, 21, 22, 38, 153, 162, 171, 172, 174
Dreier, Mary, 50
Dudley, Edith, 173, 175
Eliot, George, 37, 180
employee welfare, 5, 113, 118, 181
Enloe, Cynthia, 54

Factory Investigating Commission, 54, 79, 84, 94
Farmerettes, 103, 104
Feminism, 52, 54, 55, 99, 146, 179, 180

Gildersleeve, Virginia, 102, 103
Glenn, John, 51, 59, 67, 68, 107
Goldmark, Josephine, 4, 33, 59, 73, 86, 127
Goldmark, Pauline, 4, 94, 126, 127
Goodwin, Edward Jasper, 23, 24
Government Printing Office, 68
Governor's Commission on Unemployment Relief, 148

Gramercy Park, 127, 162
Great Depression, 146, 147, 149-159, 180
Hamilton, Alice, 145
handicapped employment, 139-45
Harlem, 24, 26, 29
Harrington, Donald, 175, 179, 180
Helsselgren, Kerstin, 131
Henry Street Settlement, 145
Hoover, Herbert, 128, 145, 146
Hine, Lewis, 46, 61
Home Relief Bureau, 151
Human factor in industry, 86, 111, 115
Hutchins, Robert Maynard, 152
Hymans, Ernst, 132

Illinois Efficiency and Economy Committee, 91
India, 167, 168, 170
International Industrial Relations Institute (IRI), 121, 125, 130-32
International Ladies Garment Workers Union, 50
irregular employment, 33, 41-46, 58, 74, 76, 87
Italian Immigrants in New York, 64, 69-81

Johnson, Alvin, 7, 12, 163

Keating-Owen Act, 101
Kelley, Florence, 4, 33-34, 102, 127, 145
Knapp, Charles, 31

La Dame, Mary, 140, 142, 144
Lasch, Christopher, 89
Leeuw, Cees van der, 131
Lehman, Herbert, 147, 153, 154
Leiserson, William, 107
Lemlich, Clara, 49, 50

Lewisohn, Samuel, 132
Lindsay, Vachel, 90-91
Lucke, Elmina, 173

Manhattan Trade School, 46, 51, 57, 162
Meyer, Agnes Ernst, 30
Miller, Alice Duer, 31
Montmort, Renée de 119, 131
Moore, Henry L., 31, 32, 42
Morris High School, 23, 24, 26, 30
Myrdahl, Alva, 168

NAACP (National Association for the Advancement of Colored People), 102
National Child Labor Committee, 34, 46, 61
National Consumers League, 94
Nebraska, 3, 7-8, 14-16, 25, 80, 99, 127
New Deal, 3, 107, 127, 129, 151, 164
New York City Employment Bureau, 94, 98, 101-05
New York Employment Center for the Handicapped, 140, 147
New York School of Social Work, 155, 158
New York State Department of Labor, 4, 157; advisory committee on unemployment, 149-51
New York State Employment Service, 93, 100, 115, 117
New York State Industrial Commission, 101, 105
Nineteenth Amendment, 4, 104, 108

Odencrantz, Frederick, 8, 12, 15, 24, 36, 38, 126, 162, 175, 179
Odencrantz, Frederikke, 3, 8-15, 17-23, 25-27, 35-36, 38, 126, 127, 161.

Odencrantz, Gustaf, 3, 8, 9, 11-15, 19-23, 25, 27, 36, 38, 126, 127, 161-62.
Odencrantz, Jeanette, 21
Odencrantz, Louise, Barnard experience, 29-38; childhood and early youth, 7-27; Columbia M.A., 44-45; director, women's section of New York City Employment Bureau, 94, 98, 101-05; executive director, Social Work Vocational Bureau, 162-65; European travel, 22-22, 119-22, 128, 153, 171; family background 17-20; family relations, 126-27, 129-30, 161; final years, 171-77; friendships, 127-29, 163, 173-75; handicapped employment promotion 139-45, 147; *Industrial Conditions in Springfield, Illinois*, 83-91; IRI (International Industrial Relations Institute), 121, 125, 130-32; investigations for the Russell Sage Foundation, 52-68; *Italian Women in Industry*, 69-89; personnel manager in silk industry, 111-19, 122-24; *Public Employment Service in the United States*, 155-57; public service during depression, 139-57; Scandinavian connections, 17-22, 153, 171; scientific management, settlement experience, 39-47; *The Social Worker in Family, Medical, and Psychiatric Social Work*, 136-39; World Conference of Social Workers in India, 167-73.
Odencrantz, Marguerite (Stockbauer), 7, 8, 9, 12, 13, 16, 17, 18, 19, 23, 24, 25, 36, 38, 126, 127, 129, 130, 161, 175, 177, 179
Odencrantz, Tulla, 8, 10, 11, 12, 14, 15, 24, 36, 119, 130, 161, 175, 179
Olson, Helen, 163, 174-75
Olson, Lois, 163, 175

Perkins, Frances, 4, 5, 53, 54, 68, 122, 125, 127, 128, 140, 146, 149, 150, 152, 181
personnel management as career for women, 111, 113
Pittsburgh Survey, 51
Potter, Zenas, 83, 86
Progressive Movement, 4, 5, 31, 33, 34, 50, 51, 60, 81, 86, 89, 102, 108, 119, 135, 162
Progressive Party, 7
Putnam, Emily Smith, 2, 30, 99

Reticker, Ruth, 129. 163, 172
Richmond Hill Settlement, 70, 74
Richmond, Mary, 136
Rivington Street, 2, 35, 36, 39, 40, 43, 45, 63
Roosevelt, Eleanor, 40, 167
Roosevelt, Franklin, 4, 40, 84, 146, 151
Roosevelt, Theodore, 57
Rotary Club of New York, 144
Russell Sage Foundation, 2, 3, 5, 47, 50-54, 59, 63, 83, 86, 93-95, 107, 111, 118, 137, 162; publications: *Artificial Flower Makers*, 60-62; *A Seasonal Industry: A Study of the Millinery Trade in New York*, 58-60; *Women in the Bookbinding Trade*, 54-57, 59, *Working Girls in Evening Schools*, 63-65

Sage, Margaret, 51
Scandinavia, 8, 11, 19, 20, 22, 119, 129, 152, 171; immigration from, 20

scientific management, 86, 111, 118, 131, 132, 135, 153
Seager, Henry Rogers, 32, 33, 35, 46, 51
Seligman, Edwin R.A., 50
Settlements, 32, 34, 35, 41, 45
silk industry, 112-15, 117, 118, 123
Simkhovich, Mary, 50
Smith and Kaufmann, Inc., silk manufacturers, 111, 114, 117, 119, 121, 124, 128
Smith College, 34, 36, 111, 138
Smith, Mary, 172, 175
Smith, Soren, 22, 168, 172, 175
Social Science Research Council (SSRC). 155, 157
Social Security Act, 107, 152
Social Security Administration, 163
Social Work Vocational Bureau, 162, 164, 165
Soviet Union, 152
Springfield, Illinois, 79, 83-91
Starr, Ellen, 35
Steinmetz, Charles, 144
Stockbauer, Marguerite, see Odencrantz, Marguerite
strikes in garment industry, 49-50; in silk industry, 112-14
Supreme Court of the United States, 114, 152
Survey, 121, 129, 153, 166
Sweden, 16, 21, 22, 25, 52, 168, 171

Taylor Society, 86, 111, 122, 128, 129
Taylor, Frederick, 86
Temporary Emergency Relief Administration, 151, 154
tenements, 1, 2, 26, 39, 43, 60, 75, 76, 87, 100
Texas, 3, 10, 14, 15, 16
Triangle Fire, 53, 54

unemployment, 32, 33, 41, 42, 45, 58, 76, 96, 93, 107, 111, 146, 150, 152-54, 157
Unitarian Community Church of New York, 175, 179
United Charities Building, 127, 162
United Nations, 166, 167
United States Children's Bureau, 100, 145
United States Department of Labor, 114, 152
United States Employment Service (USES), 105
United States Supreme Court, 59, 101.
Uprising of 20,000, 50

Van Kleeck, Mary, 4, 34, 36, 42, 46, 51, 52, 54, 58, 59, 67, 68, 93, 11, 112, 114, 115, 122, 127, 128, 135, 153
vestibule schools, 105, 117

Wagner-Peyser Act, 151
Wald, Lillian, 50, 145, 151
Walker, Jimmy, Mayor of New York, 150, 151
Welfare Council of New York, 146, 149, 158
White House Conference on Children, 145
Whiting India Guilds, 170
Women factory workers, 36, 41, 47, 52
Women's Bureau, 146
Women's International League for Peace and Freedom (WILPF), 167
Women's Land Army, 103
World Conference of Social Workers, India, 1953

World War I, 3, 79, 80, 91, 101, 120
 138, 139, 167
World War II, 133, 164, 166

Young Women's Christian Association (YWCA), 166

www.ingramcontent.com/pod-product-compliance
Lightning Source LLC
Chambersburg PA
CBHW051051160426
43193CB00010B/1139